Savanna does a great job of making sense of today's tragedies and society's quest for lasting hope. She doesn't shy away from the tough topics, and she always points people back to Jesus. In an age of self-help books she makes it clear that Jesus is the only One who can help us.

—CLAYTON JENNINGS
EVANGELIST, AUTHOR, AND POET

In a world full of pain and brokenness, the hope that we have in Christ is the only thing that we can fully depend on. In *Fierce Hope* Savanna shows us in a beautiful and powerful way how God's grace can meet us even in the most chaotic place.

—JOEL
A RAWANDAN WHOSE FAMILY HAS FELT THE EFFECTS OF GENOCIDE

# FIERCE HOPE

# FIERCE HOPE

## SAVANNA HARTMAN

CHARISMA
HOUSE

Most CHARISMA HOUSE BOOK GROUP products are available at special quantity discounts for bulk purchase for sales promotions, premiums, fund-raising, and educational needs. For details, write Charisma House Book Group, 600 Rinehart Road, Lake Mary, Florida 32746, or telephone (407) 333-0600.

FIERCE HOPE by Savanna Hartman
Published by Charisma House
Charisma Media/Charisma House Book Group
600 Rinehart Road
Lake Mary, Florida 32746
www.charismahouse.com

Unless otherwise noted, all Scripture quotations are taken from the Holy Bible, English Standard Version. Copyright © 2001 by Crossway Bibles, a division of Good News Publishers. Used by permission.

Scripture quotations marked AMP are from the Amplified Bible. Copyright © 2015 by The Lockman Foundation, La Habra, CA 90631. All rights reserved. Used by permission.

Scripture quotations marked THE MESSAGE are from *The Message: The Bible in Contemporary English*, copyright © 1993, 1994, 1995, 1996, 2000, 2001, 2002. Used by permission of NavPress Publishing Group.

Author note: All italics in Scripture quotations reflect the author's emphasis.

Cover design by Lisa Rae McClure

Design Director: Justin Evans

Visit the author's website www.savannahartman.com.

Library of Congress Control Number: 2016953077

International Standard Book Number: 978-1-62999-150-4

E-book ISBN: 978-1-62999-153-5

While the author has made every effort to provide accurate Internet addresses at the time of publication, neither the publisher nor the author assumes any responsibility for errors or for changes that occur after publication.

First edition

16 17 18 19 20 — 987654321

Printed in the United States of America

*For my comforter, Father, and friend.*
*This book, along with every other first thing*
*in my life, belongs to You. You inspired it,*
*You destined it, and You fill the pages of*
*it. Thank You for being hope in the darkest*
*places in my life. I love You.*

# CONTENTS

# ACKNOWLEDGMENTS

Tʜɪs ʙᴏᴏᴋ ᴡᴀs a labor by many. In fact, in many ways, I feel like I did the least. It took many tears, sleepless nights, corrections, prayers, e-mails, and frustrations, as well as words of encouragement and exasperation, to fill these pages. Much of what is in this book began long before the book was ever thought of. There are so many people who couldn't make this list (an acknowledgment longer than the actual book is frowned upon) whom I appreciate more than words. God has blessed me tremendously, and I am so thankful.

Matt: This book would literally not exist without you. It is as much yours as it is mine. Every dream I've ever dreamed is tied up in you. Thank you for pushing me when I needed pushing and shushing me when I needed shushing. Thank you for loving me, encouraging me, standing by me, correcting me, and believing in me even when I didn't believe in me. Mostly thank you for letting me grow up in your arms. Being a wife to you and a mom to the boys will forever be my greatest accomplishment.

August and Atlas: Being your mom has taught me more about the heart of God than any book or sermon ever has. Thank you for being patient with me while I worked on this book day and night and had only short bursts of time to play with and love on you. I love being your mom, and I'll always make time for you.

Mom: Thank you for teaching me to love others and to focus my eyes on God. You taught me to love people and to look to Jesus even when circumstances and life say otherwise. You never lost hope when things got tough, though you would have been justified in doing so. I wouldn't know the God that fills these pages if it weren't for you. Your actions and your life have always pointed me to Him.

Dad: You taught me everything I know about hard work and the value of a name. You taught me to finish what I start and not to just finish to be done, but to finish well. Growing up, I watched you work twice as hard as every other man in the room. You instilled that work ethic in me. You have always taught me to do everything I do with excellence, hard work, dedication, and focus. Without those lessons, I could never have written this book.

Mom and Dad Hartman: You have had as much a hand in my growth as anyone else in the world. You have loved me like I was your own daughter since the day I married Matt. You have taught me everything I know about prayer and the power of the Holy Spirit— gifts that this book could not exist without. I will never be able to articulate how deep my love for you is. When God brought me to you, He answered eighteen years of prayer and longing.

Kaleb: Brother, no one has taught me more about standing in the midst of adversity than you. You've never given up or quit when the world said quit. Though people have put you down, you stand tall and proud. You never let people or circumstances tell you to sit down. It was you who helped me stand when things got hard and doubt crept in. When I wanted to quit, I remembered how you didn't.

Aunt Nancee: Thank you for the lake house. This book came to life there, and I am sure many more will in the future. It's the perfect place. Thank you for always believing I could be something and never hesitating to help me make it happen.

Will: Thank you for serving our country and allowing me to make your story a part of this one. You and every other serviceman and servicewoman in this country have my deepest thanks and gratitude. I am proud and honored to know you.

Maureen: Thank you for everything. Thank you for working with me to help me write the best book possible. It was easier with you in my corner. Thank you for navigating for me, praying for me, encouraging me, directing me, and speaking life over me. You went above and beyond. Thank you for graciously answering a million questions and even more graciously forgiving and correcting my misspelling of *foreword* a million times. When I think back on this book, I will always think of you.

# FOREWORD

I MET SAVANNA HARTMAN through my brother, Rob Jones, who pastors Church of the Harvest International in Atlanta, Georgia, with his wife, Melissa. He and Melissa ministered regularly at the church in Lake City, Florida, where Savanna was formerly on staff, so Savanna knew them well and was aware that we were related. Having watched my ministry on television and Facebook, she saw that God had given me favor through social media, and when He began to do the same for her, she reached out to me for counsel about how to steward the platform in a way that would honor Him.

Savanna—now the pastor with her husband, Matt, of Banner Church in Tampa—was overwhelmed because, after posting a spoken-word video on Facebook, she suddenly had thousands of people following her, listening to every word she said, and commenting on, as well as sharing, her video. Her act of obedience catapulted her, within twenty-four hours, in front of the world. One minute she was ministering on the street and cleaning up the toys of her two little boys, and the next she was doing interviews on television and radio. God has entrusted her with a large social-media presence, just as He has me—and social media has brought us both a windfall of notoriety.

Because we have a lot in common, Savanna and I immediately "clicked." We both felt as if we had known each other forever, and since our first conversation we have become close friends. Our wonderful friendship is a God-connection for sure.

In reading *Fierce Hope*, you will learn that Savanna is an encourager. She is a voice for the voiceless—and her voice has healed many she may never meet. She has given thousands of people hope by boldly declaring that God is alive and real and in charge of what is going on not only in their lives but also in the world. He is using her because He trusts her to be Him "with skin on," demonstrating the love of the Father.

Savanna isn't afraid of scrutiny. She isn't afraid of being unpopular. She is fearless and unwilling to be put into a box. She is focused on loving people back to life. I love her and what she stands for, and I am honored to write the foreword to *Fierce Hope* because I believe in her and in the message of this book.

I do not finish many books because I need a book to capture me in the first chapter. Finishing wasn't a problem with *Fierce Hope*. I absolutely could not put it down and ended up finishing it in one day. With every chapter I found myself riveted and wanting more.

I had decided to take an afternoon off and read, and I am glad I did. There are topics in this book that I had never thought about before but that are very important. In addition, the book contains life-changing stories of modern-day people as well as stories about Bible characters whom I was familiar with because of being a preacher's kid, but somehow Savanna's telling of the stories and her pairing of them with the topics for the chapters seriously blew me away. This book proved to me that people with the worst pasts can create the best futures and change the world around them if they make up their minds to place their hope in the one truth worth living for: Jesus Christ.

*Fierce Hope* is a book full of stories and information that will completely change your perspective on life situations that have kept you in bondage. It's going to break chains off you. This book will show you that love is truly the answer, that having a relationship with God is the most important thing in life, that it is important to pay attention to your heart-posture, and that it is crucial to keep your emotions in the right place. Through the teaching, the biblical accounts, and the real-life stories throughout this book, my own hope was heightened as I was reminded of God's faithfulness in the face of difficult times, both personal and global.

—Kimberly Jones-Pothier, "Real Talk Kim"
Conference speaker, life coach, and
co-pastor
Church of the Harvest, Fayetteville, GA

# INTRODUCTION

**W**OULD YOU BELIEVE I rewrote this opening sentence two dozen times? Two dozen times I tried to find the right analogy, anecdote, Bible verse, or play on words to best articulate what it's like to be a pastor and find yourself in the middle of a crisis of faith. Two dozen times I tried, and two dozen times I failed. Nothing seemed to describe it just right. No word or phrase encapsulated what it feels like to question if you believe what you are preaching. No story or analogy came close to explaining what it means to be torn between your heart and your head, your soul and your spirit, your mind and your body.

Then it occurred to me—nothing could. Nothing could describe it because there was nothing like it.

For me a crisis of faith was a crisis of being. Who God is and what He encompasses are intrinsically a part of me. My beliefs about God were so intertwined with my being, my thinking, my dreaming, and my living that the idea of separating the two seemed impossible. For me my relationship with Christ wasn't a lifestyle; it was life itself. So imagine how I felt when I was staring down the barrel of my own crisis of faith. I was having to put my money where my mouth was, and quite frankly I didn't know if I could. Here I was, a young pastor whose job it was to bring hope to lost and hurting people, desperately seeking God for hope of her own.

I watched day after day, week after week, and month after month as injustice and suffering wrecked the world that I was called to love and serve. It hit close to home in broken relationships and miscarriages and in walking with a childhood friend—a wonderful, Christian, twenty-three-year-old mother of three—through late-stage cervical cancer. And it hit hard with heart-shattering acts of worldwide violence that robbed hundreds of people of their lives while they were simply taking a train home from work or a plane home from vacation.

I found myself struggling to understand how the loving, merciful, and kind Father whom I read about and prayed to every day could exist in the same world as airport bombings and famine. If He was so mighty and so powerful and so strong, why was He not stopping it? Why was unimaginable terror plaguing a world that He created? Why was He letting unimaginable pain impact the hearts of the children He loved? Over and over the church would say, "We're praying for you!," but what good was it really doing? The homeless were still homeless, the sick were still sick, and the broken were still broken.

I came to a place where I was asking "Why?" more than I was asking "Who?" Up until that point I had always pointed people toward who God is. In confusion, He is peace. In pain, He is comfort. In death, He is life. Suddenly one day it changed. Instead of pointing toward the *who*, I began focusing on the *why*. Why is there confusion? Why is there pain? Why is there death? I stopped focusing on the person of God and started focusing on the problems of the world.

So I became stuck. On one hand, I loved God. I had experienced His hand at work in my life. I had seen miracles with my eyes and experienced new life in Christ. I had walked in moments of great faith and lived in moments of supernatural provision. I knew God and His voice as well as I knew my husband. I knew God was real. On the other hand, I loved people. I had grown to love and care for people very, very much. It was the call of God on my life; I had built a life of celebrating with people through their wins and their joys, but that also meant walking with them through their pain and heartache. After so many trips down broken, pain-filled roads with no answers to explain suffering or words of encouragement to alleviate it, I knew evil was real too.

Not knowing where to turn, I did the only thing I knew how to do. I prayed. Well, honestly, it was less of a prayer and more of a really candid conversation with God. I mean, this was one of *those* moments in my life. You know, those fight-or-flight, turn-or-burn, do-or-die moments. The kind of moment you look back on and say, "That was the moment it all changed for me." I was at a place where I had to decide—God is real, He is who He says He is, and He has a plan for my pain, *or* God is not real, He is not who He says He is, and He has no plan at all. That day as I talked to God, I uttered a phrase that would be the start of a long conversation and life-changing revelation for me: "God, if You are real, if You really exist, would the world be this way, so sick and so twisted?" (Yes. I think in rhymes sometimes. On the side I'm a casual rapper.)

Over the next six months He would answer me little by little, and that answer would come in the form of a spoken word. Slowly but surely I would ask and He would answer. I would cry and He would comfort. I would seek and He would show me. He began to show me a world much more real than the one we see with our physical eyes. He showed me an enemy that existed before we ever took a breath, and He showed me the enemy's plan to destroy our lives. He showed me that He is as real in crisis and heartache as He is in joy and plenty. He showed me that He has a plan for suffering. He showed me that what the enemy intended for harm, He could use for good.

Most importantly He showed me that He is real, that He is who He says He is, and He does have a plan.

I should probably let you know here that I don't have all the answers. I'm not an expert on pain and suffering. I'm not a seasoned theologian, and I don't always say things in the most eloquent way possible. But I am a person. I do know what it's like to know and love God, and I also know what it is like to be confused. I know what it's like to find yourself in a crisis of faith, full of doubt and painfully questioning the existence of God.

This book isn't going to have all the answers. Based on what you're going through right now, it may not have even one answer; but I will tell you one thing: *this book is full of hope.* It is possible to find hope in the hardest situations imaginable. It is possible to find fierce hope in a chaotic world. My prayer is that once you finish this book, you will not only have found fierce hope of your own, just as I did, but also that you will feel comfortable and sure enough in that hope to carry it into the lives of hurting people all over the world.

Here is a spoken word—one God used to provide me with some answers:

Look outside of yourself and what do you see?
A world that is shaken, taken out at the knees.
We all stand waiting, breath hitched in our throat,
For a bomb in a subway, a plane, or a boat.
What's coming next? Who will die? Can it stop?
Living in fear for the next shoe to drop.
Will it be terrorists or race wars or poison?
Will it be accidental or of our own choices?
A tornado or fire or tsunami could do it.
What happens next, and will we get through it?
Stereotypes rule us. They steer our decisions.
We cut each other down with a surgeon's precision.
He's white so he's "racist"—he's black and "entitled,"
He's a terrorist "Muslim"—he's a "judge" with a
     Bible.
Prayers are just platitudes; they no longer hold
     weight.
Religions once known for love
Now spewing judgment and hate.
We don't value people, we don't care who they are.
We keep normals up close and weirdos out far.
We've declared war on the wrong things, like
     bathrooms and cups,
Forgetting people that use them want acceptance
     and love.

There are more slaves on this planet than ever
    before:
For working, for sex, to run drugs, or clean floors.
Those who used to be called on for protection and
    service,
Will they help us or beat us or save us or hurt us?
Loneliness is rampant in a world of connection.
So many screens in our face we can't share true
    affection.
Kids punch their parents and cuss out their
    teachers,
So desperate for love, having sex under bleachers.
Attention so longed for they'll shoot each other in
    school.
Drinking is normal, and drugs are now cool.
Unwed teenage mothers and absentee fathers
With no clue about words like *cherish* and *honor.*
When tragedy strikes, people start looting,
Robbing cash registers during theater shootings.
Radical killers empty gun clips in clubs,
Hopeless young mothers drown their kids in
    bathtubs.
Soldiers lay down their lives in Middle Eastern
    war zones.
They leave for deployment and never come home.
The world's falling apart. It's barely holding
    together.
The most dependable thing we have is the weather,
And it can't be predicted, and it can't be controlled:
Hurricanes are massive and earthquakes are bold,
Thunder rolls in and lightning will pop.
In part of the world it's raining nonstop.

Other parts of the world are struggling with
    drought.
Our planet is dying, all we need running out.
Excuses are given by chatty politicians.
"Global warming has caused it! It's greenhouse
    emissions."
Natural resources are dying because of pollution.
We're desperate for answers. We need a solution.
We're fighting each other and calling mean names.
Instead of working together, we transfer the blame.
We're searching for reasons to explain all that's
    happened,
To escape from this cycle we feel like we're trapped
    in.
But the truth is simple, so lend me your ear:
It's not ISIS or Muslims or jihads to fear.
It's not men and women we come against in the
    night,
But principalities and powers of darkness we fight.
Long before we were born, an enemy rose.
He had all he could want, but it was pride that he
    chose.
So down he was cast to Earth—his new home.
Determined to kill and to rob as he roamed,
He's filled our minds with trash and blinded our
    eyes,
Our integrity traded for secrets and lies.
He doesn't care for our destiny or our future
    purpose.
He has only one goal—he just wants to hurt us.
He doesn't have to work hard; we're doing his job,
Killing each other and then blaming God,

Like it's His fault we struggle, that we're down and
we're out.
But it's not God's fault that we're swimming in
doubt.
We're sitting around while the problem gets bigger.
Satan loaded the gun, but we've pulled the trigger.
It's not black versus white, or men versus women.
It's not even us against this terrible villain,
Because the battle's been fought and the victory
won.
This fool will not win; his time it will come.
He who is faithful will ride in on a horse.
On the enemy's head His wrath will be poured.
But in the meantime, please don't lose hope.
I know that it's easy, it's a slippery slope.
When things look so dark we no longer see light,
And it feels like we're living in perpetual night,
But hear what I say—there is peace in the end.
It's coming so quickly, it's right 'round the bend.
Our tears don't go unseen or fall to the ground.
He sees every heartbreak and grimace and frown.
God gets no joy from our pain, He doesn't
celebrate hurt.
We're not abandoned in suffering; He is not
deterred.
Because we are His children and He loves us so
much.
He longs for us all to know love's gentle touch.
He doesn't shout at our weakness or mock our
small frame.
In fact, He loves us so much He's called us by
name.
The world is corrupt; it's a sin-riddled land.

But that isn't God's fault; it wasn't His plan.
The enemy can try again and again,
But he cannot have us, and he will not win.
So if it's a gun by a young man gone mad,
If it's depression so great we'd rather die than be
    sad,
If disease spreads the land and kills every crop,
If right on our heads an atom bomb drops,
If terrorists come or the world starts to flood,
We can rest easy. We were bought with His blood.
All we must do is ask for God's grace,
For Him to come in and take His rightful place
As the Lord of our lives and the King of our
    hearts,
And that very instant His covering starts.
He'll go before us and stop hell in its tracks.
His hands will protect us from Satan's attacks.
You might think I'm crazy and that this isn't true,
But with the way the world is, what have you to
    lose?

# THE HURT OF THE WORLD

*Long before we were born, an enemy rose.*
*He had all he could want, but it was pride that*
*he chose.*

B EFORE WE TALK about how and where to find hope in hard situations, I think it is important that we address what caused the hard situations in the first place. To know how to move forward, we have to know why the world is in the state it's in. Who is this enemy I keep mentioning, and where did he come from? Is he coming for all of us? How do we beat him? Those are all good questions, and they all will be answered in this chapter.

But first, take a break from reading and look around. What do you see? Where are you? Are you sitting on a bench at the park while your children play on the playground in front of you? Are you reading at your desk at work even though you should be working on the proposals your boss asked you for? (Shh. I won't tell if you won't.) Are you alone in your living room, snuggled up in your favorite chair with a good blanket? No matter where you are, you can look around and see a very real, tangible physical realm all around you. You can see people interacting with one another, birds flying in the sky, and dishes needing to be washed. What if I told you that there was a very real, tangible spiritual realm that you can't see?

Right in the very place you sit in, there is a war happening behind the scenes. If I could give you special goggles to see into this realm, the really cool kind that look as if they came from a Ghostbusters movie, you would slip them on and see a world full of angels and demons, spirits and powers, light and darkness, and bondage and freedom. You would get a firsthand glimpse into the battle for your soul that has been raging since the beginning of time. I know this is kind of heavy, and if you've never heard any of this stuff, it might be freaking you out a little. I know, for it really freaked me out the first time I heard it. I can only imagine what you're picturing right now. But I want to encourage you: Stay with me. Don't give up. Press through the weird to get to the wow. I promise it is coming.

Before you can have a battle, you need three things: the good guy, the bad guy, and what they are fighting over. In this case, it's the *who* they are fighting over. The good guy is God, the bad guy is Satan, and the thing they are fighting over—yeah, that's you. More specifically, your soul. Even more specifically, your soul, my soul, and every soul that's ever existed. The good news is the battle has already happened and the victory has already been won. The bad news is the devil is stubborn and he won't quit grasping at straws. He knows he can't win, so he's determined to take out as many people as he can while he can.

Here is a spoken word I wrote about Satan and the beginning of the battle:

> Here is a story of an angel gone bad.
> His name was Lucifer, and it was pride that he
>     had.
> His body was covered with jewels of all kinds
> Made just to praise God—an instrument divine.
> But he couldn't see past his own nose, his beauty
>     obsession,
> No longer wanting to praise God but wanting
>     praises of heaven.
> Above God he desired to reign up on high,
> And through his own arrogance, was tossed from
>     the sky.
> And so on the earth he had no choice but to roam,
> Never again to return to his heavenly home.
> Gone were the days of being where the Father was
>     seated.
> He was destined to be broken, bent low, and
>     defeated.
> So with vengeance in his heart and hate in eyes,
> He set off to claim what he thought was his prize.
> When God put man in the garden, He said,
>     "Listen to Me,
> You can eat anything here, but do not eat from this
>     tree."
> Lucifer knew that they had only one rule,
> So he went to the garden to play them like fools.
> He came as a snake and said, "God's not telling
>     the truth.

This tree will cause wisdom, He doesn't want that
    for you.
Because if you are wise you will be as God is.
The knowledge of good and of evil, it isn't just His.
So, Eve, eat this fruit," he whispered to her,
In passing her lips the whole world became blurred.
To Adam she went and she offered a bite,
And thus sin came in and drove out the light.

You might not know this, but before Satan was, well, Satan, he was Lucifer. And Lucifer was an angel—a big-time angel. Check out what the Bible says about it, and don't be deterred if you don't understand it; I'll explain right after:

> You were the signet of perfection, full of wisdom and perfect in beauty. You were in Eden, the garden of God; every precious stone was your covering, sardius, topaz, and diamond, beryl, onyx, and jasper, sapphire, emerald, and carbuncle; and crafted in gold were your settings and your engravings. On the day that you were created they were prepared. You were an anointed guardian cherub. I placed you; you were on the holy mountain of God; in the midst of the stones of fire you walked. You were blameless in your ways from the day you were created, till unrighteousness was found in you. In the abundance of your trade you were filled with violence in your midst, and you sinned; so I cast you as a profane thing from the mountain of God, and I destroyed you, O guardian cherub, from the midst of the stones of fire. Your heart was proud because of your beauty; you corrupted your wisdom for the

sake of your splendor. I cast you to the ground; I
exposed you before kings, to feast their eyes on you.
—EZEKIEL 28:12–17

Lucifer is the "guardian cherub" in the passage above.
God is talking about how beautiful He made Lucifer.
He says that Lucifer's body was covered in every precious jewel and that he was made of musical instruments. He was literally a beautiful vessel made to
praise God—a beautiful, diamond-encrusted tuba man.
Then one day Lucifer decided he didn't want to do the
praising anymore; instead he wanted to be praised, so
he rebelled against God. God doesn't play that game,
so God booted him right down out of heaven to roam
the earth, and a third of the angels were cast out with
him.

Once Satan was kicked out of heaven, I suppose
he had a lot of free time to think. I figure he acted
petty for a while, tried to justify his actions, pitched a
fit, and stewed on his thoughts, getting more and more
angry. Then he decided that if he couldn't be God, he
would take what he knew was the most precious thing
to God—His children, the man and woman that God
made in His image, the two people in the garden whose
lungs were filled with the very breath of God.

Then the LORD God formed the man of dust from
the ground and breathed into his nostrils the breath
of life, and the man became a living creature! And
the LORD God planted a garden in Eden, in the
east, and there he put the man whom he had formed.
—GENESIS 2:7–8

When God made Adam and put him in Eden to work the ground and keep the garden in shape, He told Adam He had only one rule. He could have anything in the whole garden that he wanted to eat, but he couldn't eat from one single tree: the tree of the knowledge of good and evil.

> Then the LORD God took the man and put him in the garden of Eden to work it and keep it. And the LORD God commanded the man, saying, "You may eat of every tree of the garden, but of the tree of the knowledge of good and evil you shall not eat, for in the day that you eat of it you shall surely die."
> —GENESIS 2:15–17

No big deal, right? It seems easy enough. If someone told me I could have every cookie in the world, but if I ate an Oreo I would die, I would have no problem avoiding Oreos, especially if I had every other cookie on the planet at my disposal. You would think this wouldn't be an issue, but when woman busted in on the scene, things changed fast.

God decided that it wasn't good for Adam to be alone, so He decided to make him a woman to keep him company and be his helper. God called the woman Eve:

> Then the LORD God said, "It is not good that the man should be alone; I will make him a helper fit for him." . . . So the LORD God caused a deep sleep to fall upon the man, and while he slept took one of his ribs and closed up its place with flesh. And

the rib that the LORD God had taken from the man
he made into a woman and brought her to the man.
—GENESIS 2:18, 21–22

Together Adam and Eve had everything they could
ever want. They lived perfect and without sin, as naked
as jaybirds, and with their every need and want freely
provided. Isn't that the life—no bras, no belts, no shoes
or makeup...just freedom? Leave it to humans to mess
up the good life. So here they are, ruling and reigning,
when this snake rolls up on Eve and tells her that she
should eat some of the fruit on the tree because then
she will become wise, as God is.

I need to stop here a second because people always
read this and skip right over this part of the story as
if it's no big deal. When is the last time a snake crept
up in your pantry and said something to the effect of
"Yo, Sally, you should eat a bagel. I know your dad
said no bagels, but these bagels are good. Do it, girl."
I always read this and think, "What on earth was this
girl thinking, just casually chatting with a snake about
breaking the rules? No, ma'am."

So, now that that is out of the way, let's go back to
the story. Satan told Eve she should eat the fruit, and
she does. Then, when she realized that she didn't die as
God said they would, she went to Adam and told him
to eat it too. And you know what? That dumb joker ate
the fruit too, and then everything changed.

> The serpent...said to the woman, "Did God actu-
> ally say, 'You shall not eat of any tree in the garden'?"
> And the woman said to the serpent, "We may eat of

the fruit of the trees in the garden, but God said, 'You shall not eat of the fruit of the tree that is in the midst of the garden, neither shall you touch it, lest you die.'" But the serpent said to the woman, "You will not surely die. For God knows that when you eat of it your eyes will be opened, and you will be like God, knowing good and evil." So when the woman saw that the tree was good for food, and that it was a delight to the eyes, and that the tree was to be desired to make one wise, she took of its fruit and ate, and she also gave some to her husband who was with her, and he ate.

—Genesis 3:1–6

Quick side note: My husband, Matt, is a pastor, and he likes to tease that Adam kind of gets a bad rap. I mean, wives, think about it. You could walk up to your husband naked and tell him to eat dirt, and he would probably do it—no questions asked. The poor guy was distracted by all kinds of things.

The Bible goes on to say that as soon as Adam ate the fruit, he and Eve realized they were naked for the first time ever. Then they went to cover themselves with fig leaves (Gen. 3:7). Why? Because when they ate the fruit and they rebelled against God and His rule, sin entered the world and they felt shame. This is what Christians refer to as the fall of man.

Up until this point man was perfect, ruling and reigning with God and as close to God as one could possibly be. But the enemy deceived them into believing that these things weren't true. Isn't that just like the devil, to trick us into believing God is making us suffer by keeping something from us, when in reality God is keeping us from something to keep us from suffering.

> **TWEET ABOUT IT!**
> The enemy tells us God hurts us by keeping things from us, when really He keeps things from us to stop us from hurting. **#FIERCEHOPE**

## CONSEQUENCES OF THE FALL

With choices come consequences, and the consequences of the Fall weren't pretty. They ripped through space and time and affected everything from the world we live on to the very bodies that sit reading this book. They call it the Fall for a reason. It wasn't a trip or a stumble or a backslide; it was a full-blown, all-in, face-first, no-recovery kind of fall. No matter how bad Adam and Eve wanted to go back and get a do-over, they couldn't.

Because God is perfectly just, He has to punish sin. He had to punish them, not because He wanted to ruin their lives, hurt them, or watch them suffer, but because He would become unjust and unholy if He did not punish their sin. That would go against His very character and nature. He first cursed the serpent where sin began, and then He cursed the man and woman. From pain in childbirth (yes, ladies, until Eve chewed that fruit, having a baby was apparently a breeze, so the next time you find yourself doubled over in a delivery room, thank ole Eve's greedy appetite), to trouble farming and producing crops, to weeds and thorns choking out

9

the lives of the good plants, it was a mess of trouble as punishment.

But those things weren't the worst of the consequences, if you can believe it. The worst of the punishment was Adam's and Eve's (and their seed, so all of mankind's) separation from God and the reality of death—both physical and spiritual death—for the first time ever.

Before the fruit was eaten, Adam and Eve had perfect fellowship and communion (which is basically a fancy word for chill time and deep chats) with God in the Garden of Eden. They could see and speak to God just as clearly as you could see and speak to me. God came and went in the garden, speaking to them and having relationship with them. However, because God is perfectly perfect, He cannot be in relationship with imperfection. When Adam and Eve ate the fruit and broke the fellowship, they broke the relationship.

It wasn't eating the fruit and breaking a rule that separated them from God; it was that they elevated the idea of promotion for themselves above the love they had for God. They cared more about getting wisdom than the One who gave the wisdom. It wasn't about the fruit; it was about the covenant. Sin doesn't separate us from God in the idea that He can't see or hear or know us, but in that He can't have intimate relationship with us.

Imagine that you have met the man or woman of your dreams, and you are so in love with this person. Everything about him is wonderful to you, even his mess. You love the way he looks, smells, sounds, and thinks. To you, he hung the moon and the stars. Even if he is all wrecked, you still can't stop thinking about him. If it came down to it, you would pick him over anything every time. That's how God feels about us. But here's the catch. Imagine that person you love so much lives inside of a cage. You can see her, talk to her, hear her, and even hold her hand through the bars, but you can never be all the way with her. You can't embrace her, you can't lie with her, you can't make her dreams come true, and you can't meet her needs, all because the cage is in the way, separating you from her.

Sin is the cage that the enemy uses to separate us from God. Before the fruit incident, Adam and Eve were cage-free, but when they ate the fruit, the cage went up and the separation occurred. God cursed not only them but their seed as well; that means that it trickled down through every child and generation to us. We too are born into sin and separated from God.

## KEEP READING

I want to preface this next little section. The last few paragraphs of this chapter will be heavy, and then we will get into the meat of the book. I imagine that though there are a lot of Christians reading this book, there are also a lot of people who aren't sure what they believe or maybe don't believe in God at all and are just looking for a logical reason why God and pain can exist in the same world. Perhaps you're reading it because you just thought the title was catchy. There are probably one or two of you who meant to grab a SF-Steven Furtick book from this section, but in your haste you grabbed SH-Savanna Hartman instead. Maybe you're reading this because your ninety-year-old grandma, who has been on your case about your atheism your whole life, gave it to you and you're just trying to pacify her. Maybe you accidentally picked it up because you thought the title was *Fierce Floats*, and you really wanted to know how to make a killer root beer float; now you've paid the money for it and are giving it a shot.

If this is you, the next bit may be a little intense for you. I don't want you to feel as if I'm coming down on you or judging you or saying that if you don't *repent this very eve,* you can't read the book. I want you to have peace knowing that you don't have to make a decision before you read this book. In fact, I encourage you not to. If you are logical, as I am, you probably like to make decisions based on good, concrete information rather than emotion, and that's OK. So, I ask you, please read on. Even if it's weird or makes you uncomfortable or you're not really sure you share these beliefs, read to the end. The last chapter is where it will all come together. You'll then have all the facts, and I am hoping and praying (even as type this at 9:19 p.m. with my kids asleep in the next room) that your heart will be moved. You can decide then if this is the decision for you. If it's not, that's cool too. I still love you, and I hope you find a bit of hope within these pages.

## DEATH AND LIFE

Along with our separation from God, death became a reality for the first time ever after the Fall. This was not just for us, but also for animals, plants, and everything. All of our natural resources, the planet we live on, the plants that we eat—they are all subject to the curse. The earth shows effects of that. The Bible says in Romans 8:22 that all of creation groans waiting for Christ to return and free it from the curse of death. There are two kinds of death that were brought on by the Fall: physical death, as in the death of the physical human body that houses our soul and spirit; and spiritual death, as in the death of the soul that comes when you are not born again into the arms of Jesus, free from the wages of sin and death, or more harshly put, eternal death.

Physical death is easy to recognize. In fact, most of us have probably encountered it on a deeply personal, painful level. It happens the moment that the human body dies, our soul leaves our body, and the lifeless body is then left empty and buried or cremated. Physical death happens at the end of our physical life, while spiritual death happens at the beginning of it. Spiritual death is a little more complicated. We are all born into sin (remember the cursed seed thing), so we are all born spiritually dead. Let's read about this in Romans:

> You know the story of how Adam landed us in the dilemma we're in—first sin, then death, and no one exempt from either sin or death. That sin disturbed relations with God in everything and everyone, but the extent of the disturbance was not clear until God spelled it out in detail to Moses. So death, this huge abyss separating us from God, dominated the landscape from Adam to Moses. Even those who didn't sin precisely as Adam did by disobeying a

> specific command of God still had to experience
> this termination of life, this separation from God.
> —ROMANS 5:12–14, THE MESSAGE

Sin and death are separating us from God, but whenever we decide to let Christ come into our hearts and pay for the sin that is in our lives by His work on the cross, we become born again, or spiritually alive. If we live our whole lives and never come to this spiritual rebirth, we will be forced to live spiritually dead for all of eternity in hell, apart from God and heaven.

I know; it's heavy. I could feel you roll your eyes. But I warned you, so please don't give up. Hear me out. This chapter is wrapping up.

Separation and death are the two greatest tools of the enemy to destroy the creation that God loves so much. They are the enemy's weapons of choice. Every spiritual bondage that happens is fed through the lenses of these two things. If he can keep you isolated, alone, and separated from the pack, he can kill you.

Have you ever watched Netflix documentaries about wildlife? You know, the ones where a gazelle family is just leisurely chilling in the grass of a savanna when a pack of hyenas creep up out of the tall grass. The cameramen do nothing, and you're just sitting on your couch screaming, "Run, gazelle! Look left. Run! You're gonna' die! RUN!" And the gazelles just keep eating, and then all of sudden one sees the hyena and BOOM—chaos. Everyone scatters, trying to keep from becoming a two-piece leg meal for these mangy dogs. If you watch, almost always, the five hyenas don't go after five different gazelles; they go after one—together. They separate one, usually a small or sick one that is at its most vulnerable, from the pack and they take it out. That is how the enemy works. He uses spiritual bondages such as depression, anxiety, loneliness, pain, and chaos to separate us from God and the people we love. Then, in one large blow, he takes us out. That's how he works.

> The thief comes only to steal and kill and destroy.
> —JOHN 10:10

He knows that we are easier to pick off when we are surrounded by chaos, and when surrounded by such chaos, we separate ourselves from the people we love and who love us.

Suicide is the tenth leading cause of death in the United States; nearly forty-three thousand people a year die by their own hand—forty-three thousand people who felt alone, believing they had no help, no way out, and no support.[1] Even those who were close with their families and friends and whose deaths came as a complete shock felt some degree of separation and pain that led them to feel as if death was the only answer. I literally had to stop typing here and cry for a while. This makes me so sad, not just because people are dying, but because they die alone—alone in their pain, alone in their confusion, alone in their heart. I hate suicide. It is such a world-wrecking, painful thing.

That's how the enemy works. He deals in world-wrecking pain. Terrorism, slavery, racism, hate, genocide, depression, and abuse are powers and principalities of darkness that he uses to keep us bound by death and separated from the One who delivers us from crisis. Don't misunderstand what I am saying; I am not saying that a bunch of demons in human skin are walking around terrorizing the world. That's not the case.

You see, love, the unending, unchanging, unwavering love of God, cannot exist without choice. God would not force us to love Him because there is no joy in forced love. When He instilled love in us, He instilled choice in us as well. Eve chose to eat the apple. Osama bin Laden chose to have planes fly into the World Trade Center. Adam Lanza chose to shoot up Sandy Hook Elementary School. Men every day choose to abuse each other. We have used our free will and choice to wreak havoc on the people and the world we love. Regardless of our abuse of choice, God still created it because He wanted us to choose to love Him.

Whenever you choose that love, you choose forgiveness and you choose life. Ultimately those choices will cause you to find and experience fierce hope.

# HOPE IN ENVIRONMENTALISM

Natural resources are dying because of pollution.
We're desperate for answers. We need a solution.

ONE DAY IN January of 1971 two oil tankers collided near the Golden Gate Bridge, spilling a half million gallons of oil into the San Francisco Bay. John Francis watched the devastation and environmental impact that resulted. Within him a passion was sparked for the state of the world and the environment we live in that would change the trajectory of the rest of his life.

After seeing the long-term effects of the spill and losing a friend to an accident, John felt that the risks of conventional means of transportation did not outweigh the rewards, so he vowed not to drive or ride in any kind of motorized vehicle again. When members of his community began noticing him walking everywhere and refusing rides, they challenged his motives, and he found himself constantly arguing to defend his choice. A few months later, for his twenty-seventh birthday, he made the decision to stop talking for just one day. That was his gift to himself—a break from all the arguing.

He learned on that day that he spent so much time talking and arguing about the things he believed in that he missed the opportunity to listen and learn how to bring change. So he decided to give himself another day of listening. That day turned into another, and that day turned into another after that. John Francis would remain silent for the next seventeen years, walking everywhere he went. During that time he received a bachelor's degree, a master's degree in environmental studies, and a doctorate degree in land resource management. He wrote oil spill regulations for the coast guard, taught college classes on environmental studies at the University of Montana, and was made a United Nations Environmental Goodwill Ambassador—all without ever saying a word.[1]

If you had asked John Francis in the beginning of his vow if walking and not talking could make a global impact in the world, he probably would have told you no. But it was his lack of speaking that made him realize that environmentalism is about more than keeping roads and parks clean and more than studying trees and endangered species. It is about how we interact with one another and the world we live in. Francis saw that environmentalism is as much about social acts as it is about physical acts.

## WHAT ENVIRONMENTALISM IS

How about you? Do you have a house? An apartment? A room? A flat? A loft? A physical dwelling of any kind? If you do, you probably take care of it to some degree. Regardless of if you have an entire mansion to keep up or just a small bedroom you share with your fifteen-year-old sister, I would assume that you keep it clean, take care of it, buy supplies, and make sure you're not messing anything up. If you don't do all of those things, I am going to assume again that you do at least one or that you are a four-year-old super genius reading this book, because anyone over four should be doing at least one of those things in the place that keeps a roof over his head.

Environmentalism is doing the same thing but for the entire planet rather than just our little space on it. Environmentalists look at the world and the problems that are facing it and work hard to come up with solutions to those problems so that we can live a long and happy life on the planet without using up everything or making it combust from overuse.

## WHY ENVIRONMENTALISM MATTERS

You may be reading this chapter and thinking about skipping over it or wondering why it's in a book about crisis in the first place. The truth is, environmentalism is a very real, very serious concern for many people in the world. There are people all over—and you might be one of them—who fear what will happen when the earth and all its resources are used up. Some people believe the overuse of our resources will result in a global collapse and that we will all need something, but there will be too little to go around so war will ensue. Basically people believe the apocalypse is coming.

The concerns that face the earth today include pollution of water, air, and soil; climate change; overpopulation;

ozone depletion; genetic modification/GMOs; deforestation; natural resource depletion; acid rain; mining;
and overfilling landfills. That's not even all of them, you
guys. If I listed them all, this would read like a science
book. Just google "environmental concerns," and your
mind will be blown.

I am embarrassed to say that I was naive about some
of these things for far too long. I mean, I heard rumors
about hairspray depleting the ozone layer (which I still
don't understand), and I watched documentaries about
overfilling landfills with trash (did you know one
single person on average produces 102 tons of garbage
in his lifetime[2]), and I did a report in middle school
about climate change and the greenhouse effect. Other
than these things, I really had no idea. I always kind
of viewed myself in a selfish bubble of my own lifestyle. I viewed the earth as an ever-renewing resource
that was unaffected by my lone presence, which is true.
The earth is unaffected by my lone presence, but once
you get seven billion lone presences, the earth starts
to feel it.

If environmentalism already freaks you out, feel free
to skip over the facts and head straight to the hope part.
However, if you still feel as if environmentalism isn't a
scary issue, let me show you some crazy facts I learned
while researching:

- America accounts for only 5 percent of the
  world's population, but it creates 30 percent of the world's garbage.[3]

- Children make up 10 percent of the global population, but over 40 percent of the burden of disease caused by environmental factors falls on them. More than 3 million children under age five die each year due to environmental factors.[4]

- Up to one and a half acres of forest are destroyed every second. In only one hundred years it is estimated that there will be no rain forests left.[5]

- Thirteen tons of hazardous waste is created every second.[6]

Isn't that crazy? I had no idea about most of that stuff even just recently. I didn't understand the fear that came from environmentalism until I started reading and researching about it. Now it makes total sense to me. We are overusing the limited resources that we have. What happens if and when they run out? What will we do?

(OK, if you skipped down because you were freaked out by the facts—this is where you pick back up.)

## SPIRITUAL ASPECTS OF ENVIRONMENTALISM

It is important to recognize the spiritual aspects of environmentalism. First, scarcity is a tool of the enemy. It's one of those bondages we talked about before. It is a mind-set the enemy uses to keep us stressed out and worried about our lack of provision instead of focusing on the One who brings provision. Remember that verse

I mentioned earlier that said "The thief comes only to steal and kill and destroy"? Well, there is a second half to that verse. It quotes Jesus speaking, and it says this:

I came that they may have life and have it *abundantly*.
—JOHN 10:10

It is God's desire for us to live in abundance, to live with more than enough, so that we might be generous and share all that we have. The enemy would trick us into believing that we don't have enough for us, let alone anyone else, so that we live selfishly and never give to those who truly need it, once again separating us from those around us.

That's all well and good, but what happens when he isn't tricking us, and our resources really do begin to disappear? Think about it this way: If you have a box of cereal and you eat a bowl every day, it will run out after a week. If you take the same box of cereal and eat only one single piece of cereal per day, it will still run out. It will just take a little longer. What happens when our fossil fuels, coal, gas, and oil run out? Can they? What about when all the landfills overflow and garbage lines the street? What about when all of the trees have been cut down, the land is all developed, and we keep having babies and nowhere to put them? What then?

> ## TWEET ABOUT IT!
> It is God's desire for us to live in abundance, having more than enough, so we might be generous and share all that we have. #FIERCEHOPE

## JOSEPH'S STORY

Enter here a man named Joseph.

Joseph was this dude in the Bible who I really identify with. (A lot of people probably don't want to admit that, because he was super arrogant and ended up in slavery and then prison, but hey, I like to keep it real. I identify with him.) To start at the beginning, Joseph was the son of a couple named Rachel and Jacob (who is also called Israel)—you can find the whole story in Genesis chapters 37–48, but I am going to give you the condensed version. (If you do want to read it, I like *The Message* because it reads similar to a book, but if you want a more accurate translation for study, I suggest you try it in the English Standard Version.)

Jacob had twelve sons, and Joseph was the second youngest. He was also the favorite. His older brothers went out each day and worked and tended to the sheep. They worked hard, and they were what you would call men's men. They were rough, they messed around a lot, and sometimes they did shady dealings. Joseph was the opposite. He liked to be inside, he was creative and thoughtful, and he was a little bit of tattle-telling mama's boy. So naturally he clashed with his brothers. It didn't help the fact that his dad made him a beautiful rainbow coat that he wore around all the time as a giant banner of favoritism. Read the beginning of the story here:

> These are the generations of Jacob. Joseph, being seventeen years old, was pasturing the flock with his brothers. He was a boy with the sons of Bilhah

and Zilpah, his father's wives. And Joseph brought a bad report of them to their father. Now Israel loved Joseph more than any other of his sons, because he was the son of his old age. And he made him a robe of many colors. But when his brothers saw that their father loved him more than all his brothers, they hated him and could not speak peacefully to him.

Now Joseph had a dream, and when he told it to his brothers they hated him even more. He said to them, "Hear this dream that I have dreamed: Behold, we were binding sheaves in the field, and behold, my sheaf arose and stood upright. And behold, your sheaves gathered around it and bowed down to my sheaf." His brothers said to him, "Are you indeed to reign over us? Or are you indeed to rule over us?" So they hated him even more for his dreams and for his words.

Then he dreamed another dream and told it to his brothers and said, "Behold, I have dreamed another dream. Behold, the sun, the moon, and eleven stars were bowing down to me." But when he told it to his father and to his brothers, his father rebuked him and said to him, "What is this dream that you have dreamed? Shall I and your mother and your brothers indeed come to bow ourselves to the ground before you?" And his brothers were jealous of him, but his father kept the saying in mind.

—GENESIS 37:2–11

Please don't judge me because I said I relate with Joseph. He was kind of a jerk. Yikes. One day Jacob sent Joseph out to find his brothers tending the sheep to get a report. Here is what happened next:

They saw him from afar, and before he came near
to them they conspired against him to kill him.
They said to one another, "Here comes the dreamer.
Come now, let us kill him and throw him into one
of the pits. Then we will say that a fierce animal has
devoured him, and we will see what will become of
his dreams."

—GENESIS 37:18–20

But the oldest brother, Reuben, felt tender toward
him and convinced his brothers to spare Joseph's life
and just kind of rough him up a little bit. You know,
as brothers and siblings do—mean pranks. I have a
younger brother, and one time he made me so mad that
I gave him three dollars to let me tape his whole head
with duct tape while my mom slept. It was not easy
to pull off; my mom was not happy, and my backside
ended up a lot sorer than his face. It's just what siblings
do. It's what Reuben and the others did to Joseph:

But when Reuben heard it, he rescued him out of
their hands, saying, "Let us not take his life." And
Reuben said to them, "Shed no blood; throw him
into this pit here in the wilderness, but do not lay
a hand on him"—that he might rescue him out of
their hand to restore him to this father.

—GENESIS 37:21–22

The brothers grabbed Joseph, ripped off his beautiful
coat—his most treasured possession—and threw him in
the pit. But it ended up going too far, as some plans
do. The rest of his brothers weren't content with just a
little sibling hazing. So when a caravan of Ishmaelites

25

rode by, they decided to sell Joseph into slavery. In their minds they could sell him and be rid of him forever, just the same result as killing him only without being responsible for committing murder. They sold him for twenty pieces of silver and covered it up by ripping up his coat and smearing goat's blood all over it to make it look as if he had been killed by a wild animal. This way no one would look for him.

The slave traders who bought Joseph went to Egypt and sold him to one of Pharaoh's officials named Potiphar. You would think that being beaten, sold, and becoming a slave would be the worst things to ever happen to him, but things actually went really well there, for a while:

> The LORD was with Joseph, and he became a successful man, and he was in the house of his Egyptian master. His master saw that the LORD was with him and that the LORD caused all that he did to succeed in his hands. So Joseph found favor in his sight and attended him, and he made him overseer of his house and put him in charge of all that he had. From the time that he made him overseer in his house and over all that he had, the LORD blessed the Egyptian's house for Joseph's sake; the blessing of the LORD was on all that he had, in house and field. So he left all that he had in Joseph's charge, and because of him he had no concern about anything but the food he ate. Now Joseph was handsome in form and appearance.
>
> —GENESIS 39:2–6

One day Potiphar's wife came to Joseph and was like, "Hey, boy, I've been watching you. Sleep with me." And Joseph, who was man of integrity and who valued and respected his master, refused her advances, even though she made them again and again. Eventually she had enough rejection and took Joseph's coat to Potiphar and told him that Joseph tried to rape her. Without a second thought, as any good husband would, Potiphar fired Joseph and threw him into prison. The poor guy couldn't catch a break, but again you'd think this would be the worst thing, but it really wasn't:

> But the LORD was with Joseph and showed him steadfast love and gave him favor in the sight of the keeper of the prison. And the keeper of the prison put Joseph in charge of all the prisoners who were in the prison. Whatever was done there, he was the one who did it. The keeper of the prison paid no attention to anything that was in Joseph's charge, because the LORD was with him. And whatever he did, the LORD made it succeed.
>
> —GENESIS 39:21–23

Remember when I said Joseph used to have dreams? Well, while he was in prison, God gave him the gift to translate them, so people on Pharaoh's staff began to have him translate their dreams.

(If you're wondering how long it will be until I get to the part that has to do with environmentalism and how any of this relates to it—this is it. I just really enjoy telling stories, and if there is anyone you need some good backstory on, it's Joseph.)

27

One day, after a few years of Joseph hearing and interpreting dreams had passed, Pharaoh had two dreams, and he couldn't find anyone who could interpret them. Someone recommended Joseph. Pharaoh called for Joseph to be brought up to see if he could interpret them:

> Then Pharaoh said to Joseph, "In my dream I was standing on the bank of the Nile. Seven cows, shimmering with health, came up out of the river and grazed on the marsh grass. On their heels seven more cows, all skin and bones, came up. I've never seen uglier cows anywhere in Egypt. Then the seven skinny, ugly cows ate up the first seven healthy cows. But you couldn't tell by looking—after eating them up they were just as skinny and ugly as before. Then I woke up. In my second dream I saw seven ears of grain, full-bodied and lush, growing out of a single stalk, and right behind them, seven other ears, shriveled, thin, and dried out by the east wind. And the thin ears swallowed up the full ears."
>
> —Genesis 41:17–24, The Message

Joseph immediately had the interpretation for Pharaoh and told him what the dream meant:

> Joseph said to Pharaoh, "Pharaoh's two dreams both mean the same thing. God is telling Pharaoh what he is going to do. The seven healthy cows are seven years and the seven healthy ears of grain are seven years—they're the same dream. The seven sick and ugly cows that followed them up are seven years and the seven scrawny ears of grain dried out by the east wind are the same—seven years of

famine. The meaning is what I said earlier: God is letting Pharaoh in on what he is going to do. Seven years of plenty are on their way throughout Egypt. But on their heels will come seven years of famine, leaving no trace of the Egyptian plenty. As the country is emptied by famine, there won't be even a scrap left of the previous plenty—the famine will be total. The fact that Pharaoh dreamed the same dream twice emphasizes God's determination to do this and do it soon."

—GENESIS 41:25–32, THE MESSAGE

Basically Joseph went on to tell Pharaoh that God was going to bring seven years of plenty followed by seven years of famine, so Pharaoh should hire someone to manage all of the country. While the country was experiencing the years of plenty, they would grow extra, more than they needed, and they needed to store it up and collect it to be held back and used later during the seven years of famine. Pharaoh liked Joseph so much that he gave him the job, and the Bible goes on to say later in the chapter that Joseph collected so much grain it was as the sands of the ocean. They even quit counting it.

Just as God said, the seven years of plenty passed and the seven years of famine came right behind it. All of the other countries experienced drought and famine, and only Egypt had bread. Soon the whole world was coming to buy grain and supplies from Joseph.

## GOD'S PLANS

God can raise up leaders, even unlikely ones, who can make radical change in the areas that He chooses. There are people all over the world fighting passionately to save and conserve resources on our planet; some of them are so unassuming you would never know it was their passion if you just passed by them on the street. But God built them with a passion and desire to bring change to this area of the world even if right now they are too young to do anything about it.

I gave you this much backstory about Joseph to show that, even as a young teenager, God began to order Joseph's steps—even steps that looked like missteps. As a teenager Joseph was living the dream: he had everything he could want, he was the favorite, and he didn't have a care in the world. He wasn't worrying about his own resources, let alone the resources of a country or the world. But still, even then, God was preparing him to be planted and ready to take position in a role that would manage and divvy out resources in a time of famine and drought so they would never run out. God put him in place after place, like rungs on a ladder, that led him to a position where he could impact the world and its resources on an enormous scale.

God is the greatest source of wisdom and knowledge that has ever been or will ever be. When the normal brain says, "We are stuck. We have no way out, and we can't go any further," our spiritual brain says, "God can do all things at all times in all ways." God can give us plans and wisdom at any time to steward our resources so they won't run out in times of need.

I recently saw on the Internet a video of a young inventor named Boyan Slat. He came up with a creative way to begin removing the near eight million tons of plastic and trash that pollute the ocean each year. Recognizing that coastlines were where much trash collected and that they were very effective in catching plastic, Boyan went about developing floating barriers that would be attached to the sea bed in areas where trash tends to collect to act as a natural coastline; this way the ocean can clean itself, and the trash can be collected for proper disposal. In theory, this technology could remove half of the trash in the ocean in as little as ten years. Boyan is now responsible for leading the charge on what will be the biggest ocean cleanup in the history of the world. What's the catch? He's only twenty-two, and he was seventeen when he founded the company. He is the youngest person ever to receive the UN's highest environmental award. This is all because he had a creative idea to solve a problem that didn't even personally affect him. He was born with an idea in him that will impact the world and its water in a greater way than most of us could ever dream of.[7] That is the kind of God we serve, a creative, wise, and generous God.

God gave Pharaoh the dreams as warnings to prepare before either the plenty or famine ever occurred, and He gave Joseph the wisdom to interpret the dreams and come up with a plan to best serve the country in the times of plenty and famine. God didn't just reveal the problem; He also provided the solution. God is all knowing and all seeing, all the time. There is not a thing in this life that has happened or will happen that He does not know about. He can provide every idea, resource, creative whim, or direction we need to change the way we live and interact with this planet, and it takes only a moment.

## GOD IS OUR PROVIDER

Our fierce hope in environmentalism is that God is the ultimate provider, and He is a good father who wants to take care of and provide for His children. God created the earth and ultimately sustains it. His supernatural provision is our hope. He holds the storehouses to every resource in the earth, and He created them all with his hand.

This is one of my favorite verses in the whole Bible! I italicized some of my favorite parts, and it applies so well here!

> *God can pour on the blessings in astonishing ways so that you're ready for anything and everything, more than just ready to do what needs to be done.* As one psalmist puts it, He throws caution to the winds, giving to the needy in reckless abandon. His right-living, right-giving ways never run out, never wear out. *This most generous God who gives seed to the farmer that becomes bread for your meals is more than extravagant with you.* He gives you something you can then give away, which grows into full-formed lives, robust in God, wealthy in every way, so that

you can be generous in every way, producing with us great praise to God.

—2 CORINTHIANS 9:8–11, THE MESSAGE

You see that? It says He gives in astonishing ways—more than just the bare minimum! He is trampling that scarcity mind-set that the enemy is trying to keep us bound in fear of. The enemy is saying, "You will never have enough. You'll use it all up and have to fight for it. You're consuming it all." And God is saying, "You will always have enough. I'll give you what you need and then extra to give away." He doesn't just want to meet our needs; He wants to exceed them.

## OUR HOPE

The world says that you need to put your hope in conservationists. The world tells you that you need to hoard all of your resources and save them for yourself. The world says that we are going to run out and have to fight to survive, so you need to be the strongest, smartest, and most equipped.

> **TWEET ABOUT IT!**
> God doesn't want to just meet our needs; He wants to exceed them. **#FIERCEHOPE**

Our hope in the midst of environmentalism is that God created, sustains, and supplies the environment we live in. He holds the storehouse for every resource and gives out of those storehouses freely and generously.

God built each of us with creative ideas and plans to prolong our lives until He returns to reign together with us. Our hope is His goodness, His generosity, and His provision.

*Father God, I thank You for who You are. You are so good and kind and mighty. I thank You for Your promises to provide for my family and me each day. I pray that You would have Your will in all the earth. Please strengthen me that I would not be afraid or be bound by a scarcity mind-set, but help me live freely and peacefully trusting You to meet every need.*

*God, You see to it that even the birds are taken care of, and I know You love me much more than them. Environmentalism is no hard thing for You. You made every resource, and You can renew every resource. I do not fear the future of my planet because I know You hold the future in Your hands.*

*Help me, God, today and every day, to have hope in Your supernatural provision and care for me.*

*In Jesus's name, amen.*

# HOPE IN NATURAL DISASTER

A tornado or fire or tsunami could do it.
What happens next, and will we get through it?

WHILE GROWING UP, I always found natural disasters to be riveting. Because I had never lived through a large-scale natural disaster, they fascinated me. I read every book, did every report, and watched every documentary or movie about one. One of my favorite pastimes was watching *Storm Chasers* or other similar shows on The Weather Channel. This is not a joke, y'all—my favorite movie was *Twister* for about three years. You know, that one with Helen Hunt and Bill Paxton, where she chases tornadoes for a living because she lived through one when she was little but it killed her dad, so she's trying to figure out how they work. They want to put all the fancy little soda-can sensors up inside the tornado, but to do that they have to drive their truck right into the middle of it. They end up holding on to a pipe in a shed and hiding in a storm drain to survive. I was six when it came out, you guys—six. I pretty much watched it every day for a year—my poor mom. Still to this day I will watch it if it comes on television or I see it on Netflix.

I have lived in Florida all my life, so storms are nothing new to me. I was actually born during hurricane season. That's right; I live in an area that has a season for natural disasters. Because of that I have always felt very detached from the term *natural disaster*. Here in Florida we have so many storms and hurricanes that it's as much *natural* as it is *disaster*. Ask any long-term Florida resident if they are afraid of hurricanes, and more often than not you'll be met with a "no" and receive an invitation to a hurricane party. We get excited for school or work to close, to board up our windows, and to invite friends over to sleep in tents in the living room, taking turns refilling the toilets with buckets of rainwater.

I have lived through countless hurricanes, even some really bad ones. One year a tornado formed and ripped the roof right off our trailer. But I felt no personal loss from these storms, nor did I even recognize them as destructive. To me they were mostly inconvenient. This was true up until I was almost fifteen. But that all changed during the hurricane season in 2005.

## HURRICANE KATRINA

Just three months shy of my fifteenth birthday, on August 29, 2005, one of the largest and strongest hurricanes ever recorded in the United States made landfall over Southeast Louisiana. While we sat at home in Florida receiving the normal inconvenient rain and gusts of wind, people all over Louisiana, Mississippi, and Alabama were losing everything they had. Florida has seen some destructive hurricanes, but I had never seen anything like Hurricane Katrina.

We watched, helpless, as levee after levee gave way and entire cities flooded with enough water to pull homes off concrete slabs and submerge city buildings entirely. The levees that protected these coastal cities were designed to stop surges and flooding caused by a category three hurricane. Katrina had peaked at a category five soon before it made landfall.[1] There was nothing anyone could do but watch and wait.

I don't know if it was because we had family in Mississippi, because New Orleans was only a seven-hour drive from my home, or because this was the first time I had ever seen death on such a large scale so close to home, but this particular storm felt real and memorable to me. I can remember watching live news coverage of the rescue efforts with my family when, behind the reporter, a dead man just floated by, unnoticed and unclaimed. It wasn't blurred out because they didn't know it was going to happen. I had never seen anything like that before.

Of all the areas affected, New Orleans received the worst of Katrina. Over the coming days the news began to show videos of the streets and cities, and to this day those are images I can clearly recall. Lack of fresh water and power paired with dangerously high flood-waters made rescue efforts very difficult. Some people were swept away from their rooftops as they waited for help to come; some refused to leave their homes because it was all they had, and they died in the places they had always lived. As water receded, there were lifeless bodies of men, women, and children in almost every area, some covered by sheets or large pieces of trash, some blurred out, and some still being held by their loved ones. The intense flooding had caused the earth to soften and caskets to become dislodged from dirt they were buried in; they began floating down the roads in droves. Sewage that spilled into the stagnate floodwater left a smell to the city that I remember someone on television calling "the smell of skunk and decimation." I remember because I had to look up what *decimation* meant. (It basically means mass death, by the way.) If you ask anyone who participated in rescue or cleanup efforts, most will tell you that the smell was something they will never forget. I saw videos of thousands and thousands of people with little to no clothes or possessions packed into the Superdome and other areas of the city waiting for help to come; for some, that help never did arrive.

In the end, drowning, disease, starvation, and injury claimed the lives of more than 1,800 people throughout the Gulf Coast. To this day hundreds are still missing and unaccounted for. Hundreds of thousands of people were left homeless, jobless, and hopeless. The destruction totaled over 100 billion dollars. To date, it is the costliest financial disaster ever to occur in the United States.[2]

It has been more than ten years since Hurricane Katrina hit, and I still remember it clearly and vividly, as if I were still sitting and watching as it happened. I have spoken to people who lived through the disaster in New Orleans who still know and feel the heartbreak and destruction those events caused each and every day. They still hide in their bathrooms at the sight of lightning and go inside at the very whisper of thunder. They live every day in fear of being displaced, or worse, by a storm that they have nothing to do with and no way to stop. Hurricane Katrina left a permanent scar on their lives and a permanent scar on the United States.

The heartbreaking thing is that I could remove Hurricane Katrina and put a number of other famously named storms in its place, and the story would still be the same. There are stories even more personal and heart wrenching than mine all over the world, from New York to Asia. The death and destruction caused by these types of storms happens every day all across the planet. There is no other force on Earth, man-made or natural, that can cause the immediate and irreversible damage that a natural disaster can. Natural disasters have the ability to rob people of their lives, to rid people of their possessions, and to wreck the surface of the earth that they land on.

Hurricanes, earthquakes, tornadoes, heat waves, droughts, volcanic eruptions, tsunamis, and other natural climate and geophysical disasters have claimed eight million lives and caused trillions of dollars in damage worldwide in the last hundred or so years.[3] Natural disasters truly are a force unlike any other, and unlike a disaster that is man-made, they cannot be reasoned with or talked down. We cannot question their motives or speak to their sanity. We cannot ask them why they are doing what they are doing, and we cannot beg them to stop. Natural disasters are forces to be reckoned with.

## PERSONAL EFFECTS OF NATURAL DISASTERS

I imagine that if this is a very real, personal topic for you, that you're sitting on your couch with tears streaming down your face as you read my story about New Orleans (if you were even able to finish it). Now you are recalling the natural disaster that you barely lived through—the storm that you watched rip apart the home you grew up in and level the town that you loved. You know exactly how it feels to sit perched on your roof, held tightly in your grandmother's arms, begging for a boat or a helicopter to come by and see you. You remember the water lapping at the edge of the roof and how you could feel the house creaking and bowing beneath you. If the neighbors hadn't come by in their canoe when they did, you don't know what would have happened. You still have nightmares about it.

Maybe you lived through the 2013 Oklahoma tornado disaster and felt sick to your stomach reading my *Twister* anecdote at the beginning of this chapter. You didn't think it was entertaining or riveting to pull a six-foot-long two-by-four out of the windshield of your car, and thank God that it went through the passenger side and not the driver's side as you rushed to the school for shelter.

Maybe your heart is not broken because of a natural disaster, but by them, because in 2010 you went with your church to aid in missions and relief efforts following the Haiti earthquake, and your body came home but your heart stayed there. You'll never forget what it was like to move piles of rubble from the street only to find the body of a young woman trapped beneath, her arms wrapped tightly around her infant child, shielding her from falling debris. You'll never forget how your heart seized in your chest when you gave that dust-covered four-year-old boy your water bottle as he sat on a street corner crying because his parents were nowhere to be found; you told him you'd find them, but in your heart you knew he would probably never see them again. You'll never forget how it felt to see so much destruction and feel so helpless. So now your heart is to partner with companies such as the American Red Cross to aid in rescue and relief efforts all across the world as natural disasters rip through homes and highways, leaving nothing but destruction in their paths.

You guys. I am crying right now, just so you know. I stopped to read it out loud to my husband, and I'm literally bawling like a baby. This stuff is hard. It's sad. It hurts my heart to type it. I am thinking of you. Sometimes I don't know what to say, but I do want to say I feel this with you.

Maybe none of those scenarios hit on a personal level for you, but still you feel terrified and heartbroken reading them because ever since you can remember, you've had a deep fear of natural disasters and storms. You don't know why. You yourself would say that you have no reason to fear them; you have never experienced one or known the loss and destruction caused by one. You don't even know anyone who's been in one, but still you live every day in fear that the next bolt of lightning across the sky could be the last one you ever see. At night when it storms, you lie awake begging God or whoever to protect you. You tremble and cry and pray for peace, even though you've never even been to church and you're not even really sure how to pray. Each day before you go out, you check the weather, and if it even looks like rain, you make an excuse to stay home for the day. You keep a disaster kit in the trunk of your car. Even though you live nowhere near a fault line, your biggest fear is an earthquake swallowing your car up as you drive home from work. If this is you, don't be ashamed or embarrassed.

As I write this, I am staying at a family member's lake house because I have two toddlers and my life is a constant ball of noise. I came here to write in quiet. For real, I am working on this chapter about natural disasters while it storms. Last night I had to fall asleep watching Netflix because the storm noise was freaking me out. I am not even afraid of storms, but when it sounds as if lightning is dancing on the roof six feet above your head, you'll crawl under a bed really quick—no shame in my game.

## WHY NATURAL DISASTERS HAPPEN

So, where do we go from here? You're probably thinking, "OK, girl, I am reading this book to get some answers, not to relive the most painful memories of my life. So get to the point." To that I say, "You're right. Let's do this. Let's tackle the hard questions and get some answers."

As with everything in this life, there are two lenses

through which to view natural disasters: physical and spiritual.

If I were a student writing a college term paper, this is the part where I would rattle off a bunch of facts and figures and use terms such as tectonic plates or flow of tides, but alas, I am not a student and this is not a term paper. Yes, things such as shifting tectonic plates, erosion, increased rain flow, pockets of air pressure, and hot and cold fronts all play a part in making the perfect mix of environmental factors to cause natural disasters, but I am no expert on those things. If I were to go into it, you'd basically get a bunch of regurgitated Google. You would probably throw my book in the trash because it would remind you of your boring seventh grade science teacher who gave you assignments only from your textbook and never let you do cool baking soda and vinegar volcano experiments.

Insert painful childhood anecdote here: When I was in the fifth grade, I made a volcano for my school's science fair, but my mom and I forgot to put a water bottle on the inside of the foam volcano to catch the baking soda and vinegar lava. So when I put all the ingredients in, they just dissolved the cardboard box platform that my volcano was built on and it all collapsed in on itself similar to a sinkhole. It was the sad, smelliest failure in the classroom. Talk about natural disasters.

Nevertheless, I'm not the expert who should talk about the physical side of natural disasters. So let's look at them through a spiritual lens.

Remember when we talked about the world being cursed because of the fall of man in chapter 1? This is where that applies. I know it's a little confusing, but I am going to try and help you break it down.

> For the creation was subjected to frustration and futility, not willingly [because of some intentional fault on its part], but by the will of Him who subjected it, in hope that the creation itself will also be freed from its bondage to decay [and gain entrance] into the glorious freedom of the children of God. For we know that the whole creation has been moaning together.
>
> —ROMANS 8:20–22, AMP

We are responsible for the earth. We rule, reign, and subdue it. So when man fell, everything that he owned went with him.

After man fell, there were two problems. The first was that when God made man, He gave dominion (which is fancy word to say "boss powers") to us. We are responsible for the earth; we rule, reign, and subdue it. So when man fell, everything that he owned went with him.

Think of a criminal that has been arrested for robbing a string of banks—let's call him Mr. Stolen Bucks. Mr. Stolen Bucks committed several robberies over a long period of time before he was caught. Using all of the stolen money, he built a lavish lifestyle for himself, Mrs. Bucks, and their children, Nickel and Dime. When he was arrested, the things that he owned were seized so that he could not get out of jail and continue on living the same lavish lifestyle that he had before. We would all agree that this was just. In the same way, when man fell, our dominion on the earth was affected.

So what does that look like? Plant life and vegetation can now die, and not all of it is good for consumption. It can rot, spoil, and turn into a mess of tomato mush in the back of your refrigerator. Also, the earth doesn't help us anymore. We have to work hard and toil the ground. We have to till it, plant it, fertilize it, and irrigate it, and even when doing all of this, we have to hope the sun and seasons create a perfect atmosphere for growth. Many times we have success in this, but sometimes we fail.

Growing up, my dad worked in tobacco fields. He would plant, grow, and harvest hundreds and hundreds of acres of the sticky, tar-filled leaves. When tobacco wasn't in season, my dad filled the same hundreds of acres with corn or peanuts. In summer he would plant watermelons.

My dad is the hardest worker I have ever known in my life. In fact, he taught me everything I know about hard work. He would not only plant and harvest, but he would also have to watch the plants closely as they grew, checking for fungus, spraying for pests, and irrigating them without flooding them. He would leave when it was still dark in the morning and work hard in the hot sun all day, coming home well after dark sometimes, to shower and eat before going back again—especially if a storm or cold front was coming in.

Farming is not a simple man's work, as many act. It is a physically and intellectually demanding job. I promise you I have watched a lot of men do a lot of jobs, but none of them require the back-breaking, body-aching, round-the-clock attention that farming does. Farming depends on circumstances out of your control—weather, seasons, dirt, wind, and rain. All my dad could do was plant, tend, and hope it grew. Before the Fall these plants would have sprouted right up with no trouble. When man fell, the perfect system that God had built for us to rule collapsed. Instead of working with us, it began working against us.

The second problem was that sinful man could not live on a sinless earth. A world without sin would be paradise. Imagine that Mr. Stolen Bucks is not sent to prison but is instead forced to live out his punishment in Hawaii. He would get to have all the food, drink, leisure, and fun he wanted in one of the most beautiful places on Earth. Instead of spending his days in solitary confinement, he would get to lie alone on a beach with his toes in the sand, soaking up the sun. He wouldn't have to work or do anything because the land would maintain itself. There would be no disgusting lunch tray meals, because he would just live off the fruit and food that the land was naturally producing. Forget building castles of playing cards covered in aces and kings; he would be building sand castles big enough for kings to live in. He wouldn't have cellmates or bunk beds with concrete ceilings above him; instead he would fall asleep each night with the star-filled sky overhead as he swayed in his hammock. Really think about that: Does that seem fair to you? Rob a bank and go to Hawaii? No, it doesn't. It wouldn't have been a punishment for sinful men to live in paradise, so Earth became cursed as well. God is just, and justice says the punishment has to fit the crime.

Natural disasters are a natural part of both a fallen world and a world subject to physical cycles and patterns of weather.

## THE ONE RESPONSIBLE FOR NATURAL DISASTERS

If we have a good understanding of why natural disasters happen, then naturally we want to know if God causes them. Believe it or not, I am super excited to cover this question. Isn't that weird? Most people avoid this question at all costs because it is hard and confusing. No matter what you say, someone ends up upset, and they will inevitably have another question for every answer you give them. But I feel oddly excited as I write it. Don't mistake my excitement as an indication that I am the final authority, but I have spent a lot of time with God, I've had a lot of deep conversations with my pastor husband, and I think God has given me a really cool perspective on this particular question. (Plus I get to tell a lot of really cool stories in this section, and that's my favorite thing to do.)

So, does God cause natural disasters? No. He is sovereign and allows them, but He does not cause them. No matter what anyone tells you, God does not sit in heaven and think "Hmm...I am a little bored today, so I'm going to toss a tsunami down there to kill a bunch of people and watch them suffer." The God I know is loving and merciful and kind. He takes no joy in the suffering of His children.

**TWEET ABOUT IT!**

The God I know is loving and merciful and kind. He takes no joy in the suffering of His children. **#FIERCEHOPE**

How do I know that it isn't God who causes such disasters? Mark 4 records Jesus and His disciples taking their boat across a lake. It must be the biggest lake in the history of the world, because it takes them through the night to cross it. As they are crossing it, the Bible says a huge windstorm arose and the waves beat against the side of the boat, filling it with water and causing it to begin to sink. The disciples ran to get Jesus, who was sleeping, by the way (because Jesus isn't afraid of a little storm in life), and they woke Him up. This story always makes laugh because the disciples were so dramatic. When they wake Jesus up, they yell: "Master! Don't you care that we are going to die?" (Mark 4:38, author's paraphrase). It seriously makes me laugh every time. So Jesus gets up and yells into the storm "Peace! Be still!" and the storm stops and there is a great calm over the water (Mark 4:39). Jesus would never have rebuked (or said "sit down and shut up" to) something that came directly from the Father.

One time in church I heard a story about a pastor who lived in the Midwest, and a tornado touched down in his town. When the tornado was approaching his property line, he went out in his yard and pointed toward the tornado and rebuked it, telling it that it couldn't come on his property. The tornado went around his property line—never across it. Not a single thing he owned was damaged. I don't know if that story is true, but it sure makes a good illustration.

So if God doesn't cause natural disasters, who does? The short answer is Satan. The Bible calls him the prince of the power of the air (Eph. 2:2). God, in His sovereignty, allows natural disasters, but it is Satan who causes them. One really cool example of this is the story of Job.

Job is one of my all-time favorite books of the Bible, and it is definitely my favorite in the Old Testament. It is my favorite book of the Bible because it reads as a story and also because God is sarcastic in it, and I love that. (By the way, if you're new to this whole Bible name thing, you say Job like "Jobe" with a long "o," rather than "jahb," as in job interview.) So Job is named after the guy it is about, and he really loves God and lives with his family in the land of Uz. Let's read about Job:

> One day when the angels came to report to GOD, Satan, who was the Designated Accuser, came along with them. GOD singled out Satan and said, "What have you been up to?" Satan answered GOD, "Going here and there, checking things out on earth." GOD said to Satan, "Have you noticed my friend Job? There's no one quite like him—honest and true to his word, totally devoted to God and hating evil." Satan retorted, "So do you think Job does all that out of the sheer goodness of his heart? Why, no one ever had it so good! You pamper him like a pet, make sure nothing bad ever happens to him or his family or his possessions, bless everything he

does—he can't lose! But what do you think would happen if you reached down and took away everything that is his? He'd curse you right to your face, that's what." God replied, "We'll see. Go ahead—do what you want with all that is his. Just don't hurt him." Then Satan left the presence of God.

—Job 1:6–12, The Message

Satan attacks every part of Job's life trying to get him to curse God. He attacks everything from Job's health to his property and possessions, destroying it all. He sent bolts of lightning to kill his farm animals. Satan even sent a natural disaster to kill his seven sons and three daughters. Let's pick up the story. Here Job is told of a tragedy striking:

Your children were having a party at the home of the oldest brother when a tornado swept in off the desert and struck the house. It collapsed on the young people and they died. I'm the only one to get out alive and tell you what happened.

—Job 1:18–19, The Message

Natural disasters have been a tool of destruction from the enemy since the beginning of time. God allowed Satan to attack Job, but God did not cause the pain or attacks Himself. He chose to allow Satan to tempt and try Job to show that Job was faithful and would never leave God and that even in Job's trouble, he would still love and trust God. The story of Job challenges me every time I experience hardship in my life. Do you know what Job's response was when his children died? "God gives, God takes. God's name be ever blessed"

(Job 1:21, THE MESSAGE). Not once through all of this did Job sin; not once did he blame God.

## GOD WORKING THROUGH NATURAL DISASTERS

The fact that Satan causes natural disasters still poses a question: If God can stop natural disasters, why doesn't He? What was gained by Job going through all he did? Probably one of the greatest hurdles in a Christian's life, at least in mine anyway, is reconciling the fact God is loving, good, and merciful even in the midst of terrible disaster. I have to remind myself every day that no matter what happens to me, God is still working through me.

I believe that God allows storms and disasters in our lives to draw us closer to Him, to show us greater truths, and to give us opportunities that, outside of disaster, we may never experience.

Paul was an apostle (a Christian teacher/church planter) in the Bible. He actually wrote about half of the New Testament. You'll read about him a lot in this book. (But he wasn't always so good.) The story we are discussing here can be found in Acts 27 and 28.

> ### TWEET ABOUT IT!
> God allows storms in our lives to draw us closer to Him and to show us greater truths.
> **#FIERCEHOPE**

At this time in Paul's ministry (as well as a few other points), he was a prisoner who had to be transported on a ship across the sea to Rome. They had attempted to make the journey several times, but the wind and weather weren't really permitting. Paul told the ship's leaders that he felt as if the trip was going to end in disaster for both the ship and the men, but no one listened to him. As they continued to sail on in spite of Paul's warning, a terrible storm came and wrecked their world. Some theologians believe it was a storm surge or hurricane because it lasted several days. At one point the Bible says they hadn't seen the sun or stars in many days because the storm was so vast and powerful (Acts 27:20).

At this point they lost complete control of the boat and were forced to go wherever the wind blew them. When the wind started blowing them in the direction of some rocky shallows, they had to throw over much of their possessions and cargo to lighten the load to avoid hitting the rocks. Each day, as the waves battered the boat and more water was taken on, they had to throw over additional provisions.

After surviving the storm for fourteen days, the men noticed that the depth of water under the boat began to decrease one night, but because it was dark out, they could see no land. They threw over their anchors and hoped for the best. When daybreak came, they saw a bay with a beach out in front of them, so they raised anchor and let down what was left of the sails to try and run aground on the beach. Still far from shore, they hit a reef and the brittle boat broke to pieces. All of the men and prisoners jumped into the sea and swam the rest of the way.

It turned out that they had wrecked at an island called Malta. The natives were very friendly and offered them food and shelter. The man in charge of the island was named Publius, and his father was sick. Paul went to his house and laid hands on him and prayed for him; the man was healed (Acts 28:8). Over the course of the three months that Paul was on the island, the Bible says that everyone who was sick came to Paul and was prayed for and got healed (Acts 28:9).

God did not cause the storm that wrecked the ship, but He did allow it to happen so that a greater good could happen. Had God stopped that storm from wrecking the ship, Paul would have never landed at Malta, and countless people would have never experienced salvation or miraculous healings. It probably didn't make sense to the other men on the boat, but it made sense to Paul, who knew that God was in all things at all times.

## OUR HOPE

The world says we need to put our hope in meteorologists who can predict and plan the patterns of weather. The world says that we need to invest all of our money into storm shelters, because they are the only protection we have when storms come. The world says that there is no point in hoping in a greater protection, because storms will always come and we can't do anything about it.

Our hope in the midst of natural disaster is God's sovereignty. Just as Jesus rebuked the storm, God can stop any disaster at any time. At the same time, as with the hurricane that shipwrecked Paul on the island of Malta, we know that if He doesn't stop it, He is still with us and is working a good much greater than we can see or understand.

I heard Rick Warren say once that everything that happens on the earth is "Father-filtered."[4] It flows through God's hands before it reaches us, and we must find a way to trust in our hearts that if He has allowed it, He has a plan for it and He will not abandon us within it.

*Father God, I thank You that You are the voice that calms the seas. I trust You, God, and I believe that You are working all things for my good even if I don't understand it.*

*If I am afraid, I will trust You. If I have lost everything, I will hold tight to You. You hold the storehouses of the wind and snow. You formed the clouds and You tell rain where to go. All of the earth does what You say.*

*You are great and mighty, and I am so thankful that You extend a hand to protect and cover me, even if I don't see it or feel it. Thank You for always looking after me and going before me.*

*In Jesus's name, amen.*

4

# HOPE IN PREJUDICE

Stereotypes rule us. They steer our decisions.
We cut each other down with a surgeon's precision.
He's white so he's "racist"—he's black and "entitled,"
He's a "terrorist" Muslim—he's a "judge"
with a Bible.

On Thursday, July 7, 2016, at seven thirty in the morning, my husband, Matt, woke me up from a dead sleep. Keep in mind that since we have two children under three years of age, we sleep very little, so we alternate days to sleep in. Thursday was my day. I love my husband all the time, but I loved him less when he woke me up that morning.

He had good reason, though. He woke me up to tell me that he felt I should probably get out of bed because *ABC Action News* was at the door. I called him a liar. He said he was serious, but I still didn't believe him. Why would *ABC Action News* be there to see *me*? This continued for another fifteen minutes before I finally pulled myself out of bed, put on some pants, and walked my crusty face into the living room, where the *ABC Action News* people now stood. Matt was not a liar.

A well-dressed man in a suit with a cameraman behind him asked me if I had had a chance to look at my Facebook yet. "Umm...hello, bro. You just woke me up at the crack of dawn. No, I haven't looked at my Facebook page," I thought. He informed me that a video I recorded the previous day of a spoken word and prayer about the shooting deaths by white cops of African American men Alton Sterling of Baton Rouge, Louisiana, and Philando Castile of Falcon Heights, Minnesota, had gone viral overnight.

In the spoken word I commented openly about the privileges that I have experienced in my life as a young white woman. Many people confuse privilege with ease, but my life has not been easy. In fact, it has been harder than that of most people, but it definitely wasn't made harder because of my skin color.

I apologized for the mistreatment and wounds caused to the black community at the hands of some white people. No, I didn't own slaves, and I don't know if anyone in my family ever owned slaves. I have never shot or killed a person of color, and I don't know anyone who has. Many people asked why I apologized if the mistreatment wasn't a direct fault of my own. Honestly I just felt as if they were owed an apology. A lot of people told me I was wrong, but many joined hands with me.

I spoke openly about the expectation for failure of black children who are in the same educational and economic class as white children who are expected to succeed. I apologized to black men and women for our rejection of them as people but our keeping the things about their culture that we love, such as their clothes, music, and style. I addressed those who claim that systemic prejudice is no longer an issue in our culture. I opposed people who said that the deaths of those men and others were deserved because of their background, race, or lifestyle.

I reminded everyone who would listen that we all deserve death, but Christ preserved all our lives with His work on the cross.

Ultimately I called for change—a change that must begin with me, a change in behavior, mind-set, ideals, and accountability. I called for a stand for justice and love. I ended the video with a prayer and a call to action for my brothers and sisters of all colors to join with me so that our children will not have to live through the same mistakes and heartbreak that we are going through.

The reporter was there because they had aired the video on the early morning news and he wanted my thoughts about the overwhelming response. At seven thirty in the morning my only thoughts are normally "get away from me and let me go back to bed," but I reluctantly walked outside with my greasy hair in a bun and sleep goop still in my eyes, wearing the shirt I slept in, and did the first television interview I had ever done in my life.

The reporter asked why I wrote the poem and recorded the video. I told him it was because I love and value people of all color and my heart was broken at the injustice that was occurring in the world all around us. He asked if I blame anyone, and I said I don't. It is the fault of a broken system and dangerous mind-sets that are going unchallenged and unchanged. He asked if I would do it again knowing what would happen, and I said I would; I would continue to stand even if I stood alone.[1]

Now that video has been viewed close to twenty million times all over the world. I have received some hate mail, some threatening comments, and some scary insults. I have made a lot of new friends, and I have been encouraged more times than can be said. I have done more than a dozen television and news interviews that have aired all over the nation. I have spoken on more radio shows than I can count. I have been able to speak to both local and national leaders about their plans to bring change in areas of social and racial justice. I have gotten to be a part of tough conversations all over the world—conversations that, before the spoken-word video, might not have been had. I don't say any of this to brag but to demonstrate that this subject is very, very important to me and that we—my husband and our children and I—will stand together against prejudice for as long as we have breath.

---

**TWEET ABOUT IT!**

Fierce hope in God empowers us to stand even if we stand alone. #FIERCEHOPE

---

## Problems Today

I hate prejudice. I absolutely abhor it. I was born and raised in the South, where prejudice was (and still is) a very prevalent problem. At one point I attended a school that was K–12, and there were probably fewer than a dozen nonwhite children in the whole school. And this was spoken about as a good thing, not a negative thing. I grew up where the "*n* word" was a part of common conversation, and it was more frowned upon to frown upon its use than it was to say the word. I lived in a small town where, for the most part, black people lived in their section, Hispanics lived in their section, and white people lived in their section. Interracial relationships were not simply frowned upon; they were considered disgusting and blasphemous.

I even heard a pastor claim once that the Bible said a red bird should stay with a red bird and a blue bird should stay with a blue bird. News flash, dude—that isn't in the Bible! I am not sure if this guy is still alive because he seemed older than dinosaurs when I was little, but if he is, I secretly hope he picks this up and reads it one day. I still wonder where he got that from.

In the town I lived in for the majority of my teens and early twenties, it was not only a common practice but also a celebrated act for a group of twenty to thirty young men to get in their trucks, decorate them with Confederate flags, and then drive through town in a parade of hate. They didn't call it a parade of hate; they called it a celebration of history. But to anyone not in those trucks it looked just like a parade of hate.

I am not making this stuff up, you guys, and for those of you who are reading this and thinking I am talking about another time in history, I'm not. I am not in my seventies. I am not talking about growing up in the 1950s or 1960s and riding the bus with Rosa Parks. I'm talking about the 1990s and the 2000s.

Prejudice is still a very real issue in our world, and if we continue to say that it isn't and live in silence, we give the enemy more power to divide us and to rob us of our lives at one another's hands.

## JESUS'S APPROACH TO PREJUDICE

Recently, while I was at a coffee shop, someone approached me because she had seen the spoken word. She wanted to know if she could ask me a question. I said of course she could, and she proceeded to ask me why I cared about social justice so much if I was "just a pastor." I told her it was easy; Christ was the original civil-rights activist, and His blood bought all blood regardless of the skin color that housed it.

You see, Jesus did more to break down civil, racial, social, and economic barriers than any other person in the Bible—in fact, He gave His life to do so. Serious prejudice and demeaning attitudes are expressed by characters throughout the Bible. For example, they are clearly evident between the Jews and the Gentiles (those who are not Jews). In fact, the attitude of the time can be directly compared to the racial and ethnic divides that we face in the world today. In the verses below change the words *you outsiders* and *us insiders* with different races: black (or Hispanic, Indian, etc.) and white. You'll see that it will become a much more relatable and powerful statement about how He feels:

The Messiah has made things up between us so that we're now together on this, both non-Jewish outsiders and Jewish insiders. *He tore down the wall we used to keep each other at a distance.* He repealed the law code that had become so clogged with fine print and footnotes that it hindered more than it helped. Then he started over. *Instead of continuing with two groups of people separated by centuries of animosity and suspicion, he created a new kind of human being, a fresh start for everybody.* Christ brought us together with his death on the cross. The Cross got us to embrace, and that was the end of hostility. Christ came and preached peace to you outsiders and peace to us insiders. *He treated us as equals, and so made us equals.*

—Ephesians 2:14–17, The Message

Jesus didn't break down barriers only in His death; He did it in His life as well.

---

**TWEET ABOUT IT!**

Christ was the original civil-rights activist. Everything He did, He did to break down barriers. **#FIERCEHOPE**

---

Look at the story of the woman at the well. So many people read that story from the perspective of Jesus's loving her even though she had a colorful past. (Ahem, the girl had five husbands and was living with a dude she wasn't married to.) This is true: Jesus *did* love her regardless of those things. However, there is something much deeper in this story.

This woman was a Samaritan, and Jesus was a Jew. The Jews and the Samaritans hated one another; their hatred was prejudice. Prejudice is simply the idea that members of certain groups, races, or ethnicities are superior in characteristics or abilities to others. The Jews viewed the Samaritans as half-breeds. They were thought of as lowly, and Jews avoided them at all costs. In fact, if a Jew was traveling, he would go the long route on the east side of Jordan to avoid even going through Samaria. If a Jew absolutely had to travel through Samaria, he would hasten through it, you know, similar to what you do when you see someone in Walmart you don't want to talk to. You tuck your arms in, dip your head down, and quickly scoot down the detergent aisle hoping she doesn't see you on the way to the cereal.

The Bible says that when Jesus left Judea and began His journey back to Galilee, He needed to go through Samaria:

> He left Judea and departed again for Galilee. And he had to pass through Samaria.
>
> —John 4:3–4

As if going through Samaria wasn't enough of an issue, Jesus doesn't just not hasten. He stops and sits down to get a drink. It was around noon, and there was a Samaritan woman there drawing her own water. He doesn't only get water at the same place where she gets water; He goes a step further by speaking to her and asking her to get water for Him.

> A woman from Samaria came to draw water. Jesus
> said to her, "Give me a drink."
>
> —JOHN 4:7

The woman is a little freaked out because Jews *did not*
speak to Samaritans. Jesus was literally breaking down
every social barrier that existed between the Jews and
the Samaritans, not only by sitting with her but also by
speaking with her.

> The Samaritan woman said to him, "How is it
> that you, a Jew, ask for a drink from me, a woman
> of Samaria?" (For Jews have no dealings with
> Samaritans.)
>
> —JOHN 4:9

Then Jesus responds and goes on to have a conversation with her that would not only change her life
but would also result in her becoming one of the first
female evangelists ever:

> Jesus answered her, "If you knew the gift of God,
> and who it is that is saying to you, 'Give me a drink,'
> you would have asked him, and he would have given
> you living water." The woman said to him, "Sir, you
> have nothing to draw water with, and the well is
> deep. Where do you get that living water? Are you
> greater than our father Jacob? He gave us the well
> and drank from it himself, as did his sons and his
> livestock." Jesus said to her, "Everyone who drinks
> of this water will be thirsty again, but whoever
> drinks of the water that I will give him will never
> be thirsty again. The water that I will give him
> will become in him a spring of water welling up to

eternal life." The woman said to him, "Sir, give me this water, so that I will not be thirsty or have to come here to draw water."

Jesus said to her, "Go, call your husband, and come here." The woman answered him, "I have no husband." Jesus said to her, "You are right in saying, 'I have no husband'; for you have had five husbands, and the one you now have is not your husband. What you have said is true." The woman said to him, "Sir, I perceive that you are a prophet. Our fathers worshiped on this mountain, but you say that in Jerusalem is the place where people ought to worship." Jesus said to her, "Woman, believe me, *the hour is coming when neither on this mountain nor in Jerusalem will you worship the Father. You worship what you do not know; we worship what we know, for salvation is from the Jews. But the hour is coming, and is now here, when the true worshipers will worship the Father in spirit and truth, for the Father is seeking such people to worship him.* God is spirit, and those who worship him must worship in spirit and truth." The woman said to him, "I know that Messiah is coming (he who is called Christ). When he comes, he will tell us all things." Jesus said to her, "I who speak to you am he."

—John 4:10–26

Jesus explains to her that He is the well of living water and that if she accepts salvation, her life will be changed. After hearing this, the first thing she thinks is that who she is, a Samaritan, will stop her from what He has. Jesus tells her that who she is, what she looks like, what her name is, where she lives does not matter, but the way she lives for and worships God is all that matters. This is true for you too: your social, physical, racial, economic, or geographical labels do not matter; it is the way you live for and worship God that matters.

Jesus spends time at the well to tell this woman that life doesn't label her—love does. The disciples clearly didn't get the memo, because they made stank faces at her when they rolled up.

> Just then his disciples came back. They marveled that he was talking with a woman, but no one said, "What do you seek?" or, "Why are you talking with her?"
>
> —JOHN 4:27

Remember that thing about her becoming the first female evangelist? It began with this woman's next actions:

> So the woman left her water jar and went away into town and said to the people, "Come, see a man who told me all that I ever did. Can this be the Christ?" They went out of the town and were coming to him.
>
> —JOHN 4:28–30

She told everyone she knew, and they listened to her:

> Many Samaritans from that town believed in him because of the woman's testimony, "He told me all that I ever did." So when the Samaritans came to him, they asked him to stay with them, and he stayed there two days. And many more believed because of his word. They said to the woman, "It is no longer because of what you said that we believe,

for we have heard for ourselves, and we know that
this is indeed the Savior of the world."

—JOHN 4:39–42

If Jesus had allowed prejudicial or racial mind-sets
and behaviors to stop Him from going into Samaria that
day, that woman's life would never have been changed,
she would never have become an evangelist, and countless men and women would not have received the gift
of salvation. Jesus didn't shy away from tough conversations. He didn't keep silent during racial tensions. He
waded right into the thick of it and built bridges of
unity and love where judgment and hate had built walls
of separation.

I have shared this thought before and been met with
statements such as, "I'm not Jesus. He was perfect. You
can't expect me to always act like Jesus." Well, I have
good news. There is another story in the Bible in which
a regular, sinful, imperfect human did the same thing
Jesus did—reach out to a person others ignored and
turned their backs on—and Jesus uses it as a lesson for
others.

One day Jesus was out teaching when a lawyer stood
up and challenged Him. Some translations say "lawyer"
and others say "religious scholar." Regardless of which it
is, props to Jesus for taking this on. I have friends who
are both lawyers and religious scholars, and they know
how to win an argument, even if they are dead wrong.
If I had been in Jesus's place, I probably would have said
something to the effect of "Umm...see me after class,"
and handled it in private because I would have expected

such an educated person to try to trip me up. But, in true Jesus fashion, Jesus dove right in. The lawyer wanted to know what he had to do to receive eternal life. Jesus essentially said, "You're a lawyer. What does the law say to do?" (Luke 10:26). The lawyer responded:

> You shall love the Lord your God with all your heart and with all your soul and with all your strength and with all your mind, and your neighbor as yourself.
>
> —LUKE 10:27

Jesus responded by basically saying, "OK, good. Go do that" (Luke 10:28). The lawyer, primed and ready to argue, looking for a loophole, asks, "And who is my neighbor?" (Luke 10:29). So Jesus answers with a story. (By the way, Jesus did not usually just give a straight answer. Normally He took the route of a high school language arts teacher and told a story; it was the listener's responsibility to pull the lesson from it.) So Jesus tells the story of the good Samaritan. You can find the story in Luke 10:30–35, but I'm going to paraphrase it because I really like telling stories and it's a fairly easy story to retell.

One day a man, we will call him Mr. Jones, went on a walk from Jerusalem to Jericho. On his way some thieves mugged him. They beat him, robbed him, and left him naked and half dead on the side of the road. That same day a priest, whom we will call Mr. Snob, was traveling down that same road. When he saw Mr. Jones lying naked and near-dead on the side of the road, he went to the opposite side and passed him by, offering no help at all. Later that day a Levite, whom we will call Mr. Snob Number Two, passed by the beaten man and looked but still walked to the other side of the road and passed him by. Still later that day, a Samaritan man we will call Good Sam walked down the same road and saw Mr. Jones. Good Sam went to him and had compassion. He picked him up, bandaged his wounds, placed him on the back of his horse, and took him to a hotel to take care of him. The next day Good Sam had to leave, but he gave the hotel manager a little money and told him to look after Mr. Jones until he returned. He promised that if it cost the hotel manager more than the amount he gave him, he would be sure to repay him.

The story is significant because Jesus was addressing social classes within the parable. Priests were the highest in the social order. They rode animals rather than walking. (Walking was for poor people.) They also were limited in whom and what they could come in contact with because they had to stay ceremonially clean. Had Jesus asked someone outside the example who the neighbor was in this parable, who the person they should be loving was, the response probably would have been the priest. Levites were assistants to the priests, which made them of a lower social class than a priest but still not the lowest class. Samaritans were, as I said earlier, half-breeds and the lowest of the low of social classes. Although all three men were of separate social classes, they were all three bound by the same law. All of them risked defilement by aiding the beaten man, but it was only the Samaritan who thought the risk was worth it.

> ### TWEET ABOUT IT!
> Jesus walked in love into the middle of tense situations and let love make the stand.
> #FIERCEHOPE

After telling the story, Jesus turned back to the lawyer. "Which of these three, do you think, proved to be a neighbor to the man who fell among the robbers?" (Luke 10:36). The lawyer replied, "The one who showed him mercy." Then Jesus said to him, "You go, and do likewise" (Luke 10:37).

Both examples, Jesus's speaking to the Samaritan woman at the well and the Samaritan man's helping the beaten man on the road to Jericho, are biblical examples of breaking down racial, ethnic, and socioeconomic barriers that prevent us from having full, healthy, and thriving relationships with the people we come into contact with. Jesus didn't loot any stores. He didn't burn down any buildings. He didn't stand on any cars. He just walked in love into the middle of tense situations and let love make the stand. We are encouraged to do the same. We have one rule for how to receive eternal life: love. We must love God. We must love ourselves. We must love people. Prejudice is a direct contradiction to this rule.

## LOVE BREEDS LOVE

Michael King Sr. became the lead pastor of Ebenezer Baptist Church in 1931. As a young black man with a family and the pastor of a growing church, he made it a mission to fight against racial stereotypes and combat the prejudices he saw every day in the world and in ministry. He did not fight these battles and stand against injustice because he was a black man but because he believed that racism and segregation were offensive to the heart and will of God. He raised his children to treat everyone with love and respect regardless of their color or class. He did not know it then, but he was making an impression on his son, Michael King Jr., who would go on to make an impression on the world. You and I know of Michael King Jr. by the more popular name, Martin Luther King Jr.[2]

Many people remember Martin Luther King Jr. as a Nobel Peace Prize–winning, civil-rights activist, but he was first and foremost a pastor. Like his father before him, he believed strongly in the heart of God for unity and love among people of all colors and classes. He had a doctorate in theology, and it was his faith and his knowledge of and closeness to the heart of God that inspired his activism. The reason he led only nonviolent protests was because he believed in loving one's enemy into changing, not hating him into it. This is an excerpt from one of his sermons:

> Now there is a final reason I think Jesus says, "Love your enemies." It is this: that love has within it a redemptive power. And there is a power there that eventually transforms individuals....Just keep being friendly to that person....Just keep loving them, and they can't stand it too long. Oh, they react many ways in the beginning....They react with guilt feelings, and sometimes they'll hate you a little more at that transition period, but just keep loving them.

And by the power of your love they will break down
under the load. That's love, you see. It is redemptive,
and this is why Jesus says love. There is something
about it that builds up and is creative. There is something about hate that tears down and is destructive.[3]

Martin Luther King Jr. knew how to walk and stand
for justice without standing against a person. He knew
that hate breeds more hate. I hate prejudice. And I hope
my hatred of it breeds more hatred for it. But ultimately
I love people, and I hope my love of people breeds more
love of people.

## OUR HOPE

The world says that we should put our hope in civil-
rights activists. The world says that it is only civil-rights
activists who can make a difference. The world says that
we should put our hope in political leaders to fix this
and that it's a government issue and not a people issue.
The world says we don't even need hope in this area
because prejudice and racism are nonissues.

Our hope in the midst of prejudice is this: we were
all made in the image of God. His hands formed each
and every hand that holds this book or reads these words.
He knows us so intimately and created us so intention-
ally that He knows all the hairs on our heads. He cares
more for the hearts in our chests than for the color on
our arms. He loves us so much that He sent His Son to
die in our place. He didn't die just for white people. He
didn't die just for black people. He died for *all* people.
He was not deterred by race, color, or creed. His love

stretched across the borders of skin and class and made a way for us to live free to love one another. If He could love a woman living in sin, a woman who was of the lowest social class and the most despised people group, right where she was in life, then I can love my neighbor, as the good Samaritan did, even if everyone tells me that I shouldn't.

*Father God, I thank You for loving and creating every person of every class and color. I am so thankful that Your love knows no bounds. Thank You for sending Your Son to die in place of all of us regardless of our skin color or class.*

*God, I am thankful that in You we have unity. I am thankful that before Christ all ethnicities are the same.*

*God, I ask for forgiveness for any time in my life that I have caused disunity among my brothers and sisters of any race, ethnicity, or class by my actions, thoughts, or words. Help me forgive in my heart those who have brought disunity into my life because of their actions, thoughts, or words.*

*As I move forward, empower me to bring healthy, righteous change. Help me to be an ambassador for hope, love, and unity in Your kingdom and in the world in which I live.*

*In Jesus's name, amen.*

# 5

# HOPE IN SLAVERY

There are more slaves on this planet than ever before:
For working, for sex, to run drugs, or clean floors.

WANTED TO START this chapter with a story. I wanted
to share with you the harrowing tale of someone who
had no hope or future until she was rescued from
slavery. I wanted to tell a story to show you God's
goodness and faithfulness throughout her captivity. But
instead I sit at the table, computer open in front of me,
with head in my hands and I weep.

Here I am, having coffee at the lake house kitchen
table with the windows open, listening to nature sounds
and feeling the sun's warmth through the window as
I write. At the bottom of the grassy, green-tree covered hill the house is perched on, the crystal-clear lake
water is shining like glass, and I am watching a video
of a young woman talk about how her captor threatened
to beat her in the face with an iron if she didn't make
him enough money. Suddenly the weight of what I am
watching creeps into the kitchen and sits down right on
my chest. It feels like an elephant.

Suddenly I am no longer sitting at the kitchen table having coffee and watching a video, but instead I am sitting at a coffee shop watching Natalia on what she thinks is a really great first date. What she doesn't know is that when she goes to the bathroom, her perfectly charming man puts something in her coffee. I watch in horror as she comes back and they laugh and talk some more. He encourages her to have more of her coffee. She does. I watch as her laugh begins to grow quieter and her eyes begin to sparkle less. She complains of being tired, and he tells her it's OK. She passes out, and I watch him pick her up and carry her out. When no one is looking, he crams her into his trunk as if she is old airport luggage. I can imagine the horror, the panic she feels when she wakes up chained to a bed in another country. For two weeks she lies chained and abused until she is sold as a sex slave.[1]

I am trying hard not to imagine what happens after this.

The sounds of nature have turned into the sounds of yelling and insults. I no longer feel peace from the sun's warmth; instead it feels like an enormous weight on my skin.

I imagine that's how the sun felt to Myint Thein when he was a slave on a Thai fishing boat. When he paid a middleman to smuggle him across the border so he could try to get a job, he didn't know he was actually being sold to a fishing boat captain who would smash all of his teeth out, feed him a bowl of rice per day, and force him to work twenty hours every day. Each time the sun peeks out from behind the clouds, I think about how much he must have despised the sun after two years of being forced to work for no pay beneath it catching the fish and shrimp that you and I pay thirty dollars a plate for at dinner.[2]

I look out of my window and no longer see warm, crystal-clear lake water. Instead I see the cold, gray, frigid ocean, where a young Russian girl was crammed with sixty other girls into an old shipping container. I can imagine the fear and pain she experienced as she watched more than half of the other girls die right beside her in that container. After surviving her journey, she was locked in an apartment and raped day after day until Greek authorities raided the brothel where she was being held against her will, where she was forced to service anyone any way they wanted. I feel her confusion when, as she was rescued, she asked only one question to the woman who sat before her: "Why didn't you come sooner?"[3]

The green, grassy, tree-covered hill that the house sits on is no longer a place for picnics and fun with my two sons. Instead I only see the dirty, tree-covered cocoa field on the Ivory Coast where two young boys not much older than my own sons carry machetes and baskets bigger than they are. They have been forced to work in these fields since they were young, harvesting cocoa beans from sunup to sundown. I can feel the longing they feel as they tell me they will never play or go to school. As a mother I want to reach out and hold them. I want to put them in school and teach them how to read. I want to give them shoes for their feet and bandages for their badly damaged hands. But they want nothing to do with me, or anyone well off. In fact, they hate us. The anger in their eyes is palpable when they say that the chocolate that we enjoy each time we want a special treat was made by their suffering. "They are eating my flesh," one boy says.[4]

## MODERN-DAY SLAVERY

While every topic in this book is heavy, there has not been one that has been harder for me to get through than this one. The weight of slavery is so heavy. If you were to poll one hundred people in the United States and ask them what they thought about slavery, more than likely they would think you were talking about the slavery that existed two hundred years ago in cotton fields and wealthy plantation houses. The heartbreaking truth is that there are more slaves worldwide today, in 2016, than there ever have been in the history of the world. I read some statistics that quoted the number of people in forced labor or sexual slavery as low as 30 million or as high as 45 million.[5] The truth is, no one really knows. If we could count them all, we could save them all. But we can't. Only 1 to 2 percent of forced slaves are rescued in their lifetime.[6]

What used to be called slave trade is now called human trafficking, and it is the fastest-growing criminal industry in the world. At this time it is third only to guns and drugs, but it is gaining popularity in the crime industry, because unlike drugs, a slave can be sold multiple times without losing any value.[7] Sometimes they can even be resold for more depending on how well they were trained.

I just have to stop here to say that the last sentence cost me about an hour of writing time and enough tears to fill a small bucket. The fact that any God-created human being with a heartbeat can be trained and resold like a dog rips me to shreds. The fact that there are God-created human beings with a heartbeat that not only participate in but also lead others into this kind of life fills me with this mixture of rage and hurt and, well, compassion, believe it or not. How far have these people fallen that a life holds no value to them except what someone is willing to pay for it?

Over one quarter of slaves today are children under the age of eighteen.[8] The average age of a trafficking victim is twelve to fourteen years old.[9] Over half of all slaves are women and girls.[10] The majority of trafficked humans in the world are sexual slaves, and the rest are forced to work in fields, mines, factories, kitchens, service industries, fishing boats, and homes.[11]

## OUR PART

It is easy to feel detached from slavery. I mean, we don't own any slaves. I, and probably you, have never even paid someone to clean the house. But the harsh reality is that we have participated in slavery, even without our knowing, at least once a day for the majority of our lives.

The chocolate in the candy bar you ate after lunch might have been harvested by a seven-year-old boy who was sold by his parents and forced to work in cocoa fields in Ghana. The shoes you wore this morning to the gym could have been stitched together by a sixty-eight-year-old homeless woman who was promised shelter but instead is now forced to work without pay each day for the rest of her feeble life. If you have ever purchased or watched pornography, you have had a hand in sexual slavery. Sure, the girl in the video looks as if she's having a great time, but what you don't know is that she begs for death, something she will come to experience at the hands of her pimp if she no longer agrees to be in those movies. The shrimp in the saffron risotto you had at dinner tonight might have been caught by a thirty-six-year-old man who went to school to be a doctor in Thailand but was kidnapped when traveling by boat to a new job and is now forced to work on a fishing boat catching shrimp to be sent the United States and United Kingdom.

I know these are harsh, heartbreaking realities, but it doesn't make them untrue. Those people in slavery are wives, sons, daughters, husbands, mothers, and fathers, just like you and me.

## A TOOL OF THE ENEMY

Slavery is one the darkest and vilest tools of the enemy. He uses it every day and in every way. An even more heartbreaking but real truth is that, though we likely will never be sold into sexual slavery or forced to work in a field, many of us are slaves as well. We live in bondage (which is just a fancy word for being bound and trapped). We live as slaves to sin and death without ever taking hold of the keys that are available to us to bring freedom and restore hope to our lives. God sent His own Son to the cross so that we would no longer be slaves to sin and death. When Christ died on the cross,

He busted open hell and took back the keys that the enemy used to imprison us.

> Jesus said to the Jews who had believed him, "If you abide in my word, you are truly my disciples, and you will know the truth, and the truth will set you free." They answered him, "We are offspring of Abraham and have never been enslaved to anyone. How is it that you say, 'You will become free'?" Jesus answered them, "Truly, truly, I say to you, everyone who practices sin is a slave to sin. The slave does not remain in the house forever; the son remains forever. So if the Son sets you free, you will be free indeed."
> —JOHN 8:31–36

---

**TWEET ABOUT IT!**

When Christ died on the cross, He busted open hell and took back the keys the enemy used to imprison us. **#FIERCEHOPE**

---

The enemy would have us remain trapped in sin and death, slaves to bondage for the rest of our lives. He uses tools that we've talked about in this book—war, slavery, isolation, depression, racism, and pain—to keep us alone, to keep our spirits broken, to keep our hearts hard. If we continue to blame God for the pains of this world instead of facing the enemy and breaking free from the weight of sin and death, we will remain chained in bondage and pain in this life and in eternity.

## SPIRITUAL SLAVERY

It is so important that we see spiritual slavery for what it is. Things that the world would tell us are normal, natural, everyday feelings and experiences can actually be powerful traps set by the enemy to keep us slaves to darkness.

Maybe you lived a happy, joy-filled life until you were seventeen. Something that year changed. Your mom said you were just being melodramatic, but it wasn't that. You weren't sure what caused it, but suddenly you became truly, deeply sad. There is no real reason for it, but every day you live under the weight and cloud of depression. It affects your job, your family, and your relationships, but still you cannot shake it. Depression is a bondage of the enemy; you are living in spiritual slavery.

Maybe you have lived with insecurity your whole life. Since you were a little girl, as young as six, you can remember standing in front of the mirror picking out all the things you hated about yourself. You have always been too fat or too thin—never just right. When you look at your face, you see a too big nose and too small ears. You have never had a successful relationship because you can never see you the way that others see you. You can't love anyone else because you don't love yourself. Insecurity is a bondage of the enemy; you are living in spiritual slavery.

Maybe you were fit and healthy your entire life, an athlete even. But you started feeling sick around your fortieth birthday. Now, six years later, it seems as if you're always sick. No matter what you do, you can never really get well. First it was summer colds, then sinus infections, then joint pain, and then stomachaches. Next it was debilitating headaches that stopped you from getting out of bed. Eventually you had to leave your job because you were too sick to function. You've been to doctor after doctor who can't explain what is going on, but still each provides you with a new medicine with a new set of side effects. Sickness is a bondage of the enemy; you are living in spiritual slavery.

Don't get me wrong—I don't go shouting down the devil every time I get sick or sad. There are normal life occurrences that are not spiritual slavery. However, things that are continual, unchanging, and life-killing that you cannot seem to shake are spiritual bondages.

A good way to tell if what you are experiencing is a spiritual bondage or just a life interruption is to apply the verse below to your problem:

> The thief comes only to steal and kill and destroy. I came that they may have life and have it abundantly.
> —John 10:10

If there are things in your life that are stealing your dreams, killing your relationships, or destroying your life, those things are spiritual bondages from the enemy.

Getting sad because you lost your job is not spiritual slavery, but staying so sad that you can't get another job is. Getting bummed out because you can't zip a size 6 dress is not spiritual slavery, but developing an eating disorder so you can zip a size 6 is. Getting a headache from starting at your phone too long is not spiritual slavery, but getting a headache that lasts for six weeks may be.

Just as John 8:36 says, if the Son sets you free, you are free indeed. If you are an unbeliever experiencing these bondages, you need only ask Christ to come into your heart and set you free. (You will get the opportunity at the end of this book to do so, but you're more than welcome to go ahead and do it now.) The Bible says Jesus came to set the captive free:

> The Spirit of the Lord is upon me, because he has anointed me to proclaim good news to the poor. He has sent Me to proclaim liberty to the captives and recovering of sight to the blind, to set at liberty those who are oppressed.
>
> —Luke 4:18

If you are already a believer and you are finding yourself experiencing these things, you need to rebuke the enemy, you need to take authority over your body and life, and you need to experience deliverance. It is God's will that you be free of these bondages.

## Setting the Captives Free

It is the heart of God to see every person free and delivered from both spiritual and physical slavery. He has done so since the beginning of time. Take a look at this story about a man named Moses.

Moses was born in Egypt at a time when Pharaoh made a decree that every Hebrew baby boy born was to be killed. Obviously Moses's mother didn't want to kill him, so she hid him in secret until she could no longer hide him anymore. Moses was three months old when his mother placed him in a little basket and floated him down the Nile.

She was a brave woman, because she was literally floating her baby boy in the direction of the man who wanted him dead. I wonder, as a mother, if this woman wept and prayed to God that her son would be found and kept and not found and killed. She ran that risk when she set him afloat. I guess for her the risk was worth the reward. I don't know if it was a risk I would have taken. However, her risk paid off.

Baby Moses floated right up to the reeds where Pharaoh's daughter was bathing. When the woman opened the basket and saw Moses, the Bible says her heart went out to him and she kept him, adopted him, and raised him.

Moses knew that he was a Hebrew and was blessed to be in the house of Pharaoh, but all around him Hebrews were enslaved in the millions by Pharaoh. One day he saw an Egyptian worker hit a Hebrew slave, and in a fit of rage he killed him. He fled and lived away from Egypt for many years. (See Exodus 2–3.)

One day Moses happened upon a burning bush. God was in the bush, and He spoke to Moses:

> Then the LORD said, "I have surely seen the afflic-tion of my people who are in Egypt and have heard their cry because of their taskmasters. I know their sufferings, and I have come down to deliver them out of the hand of the Egyptians and to bring them up out of that land to a good and broad land, a land flowing with milk and honey, to the place

of the Canaanites, the Hittites, the Amorites, the Perizzites, the Hivites, and the Jebusites. And now, behold, the cry of the people of Israel has come to me, and I have also seen the oppression with which the Egyptians oppress them. Come, I will send you to Pharaoh that you may bring my people, the children of Israel, out of Egypt."

—Exodus 3:7–10

God cares about the entrapment of His people. Slavery breaks His heart, and He wants to see people free from it. The Bible said that He was moved by His people's cries for help and decided to deliver them and that He employed the help of Moses to do it.

Moses goes to Pharaoh and asks for the release of his people. Pharaoh, of course, says no, and then makes a point to work the slaves even harder to spite God and Moses. Moses is distraught because he feels as if the Hebrews have it even worse because of his actions, so God tells him to go and encourage the Hebrews, saying to them, "I am the Lord, and I will bring you out from under the burdens of the Egyptians, and I will deliver you from slavery to them, and I will redeem you" (Exod. 6:6).

Again and again Moses went to Pharaoh and requested the release of his people on behalf of God, and time and time again he was met with a "no." So God told Moses to tell Pharaoh that until he freed the slaves, He would send plagues to Egypt. Pharaoh still didn't listen; the Bible says that he was a stubborn man. So God struck Egypt with ten plagues:

- Water turned to blood

- Swarms of frogs (Literally, you guys, this would kill me. It is my worst nightmare. Frogs are the only animals I am afraid of.)

- Swarms of gnats

- Swarms of flies

- Death of all livestock

- Boils

- Thunder and hail from heaven (At this point Pharaoh actually had enough and decided to release the slaves, but when he saw that God stopped the thunder and hail, he changed his mind and kept them after all.)

- Swarms of locusts

- Darkness over the land

- Death of the firstborn (It is interesting that this is the plague that moved the heart of Pharaoh. If you remember the beginning of the story, it was the ancestor of Pharaoh who called for all Hebrew sons born to be killed that nearly took the life of Moses.)

These might seem like extreme punishments for the simple release of people, but God will go to extremes to see His children free.

When Pharaoh's son died that night, he had enough.

He told Moses to go and to take the slaves with him and never return. With the help of God, Moses took nearly three million people and led an exodus out of Egypt. While they were traveling, Pharaoh again changed his mind and decided to come after them. Moses and the people came to the Red Sea. They had nowhere to go, and Pharaoh and his armies were right on their tail. So God does the unimaginable:

> Then Moses stretched out his hand over the sea, and the LORD drove the sea back by a strong east wind all night and made the sea dry land, and the waters were divided. And the people of Israel went into the midst of the sea on dry ground, the waters being a wall to them on their right hand and on their left.
> —EXODUS 14:21–22

When the Egyptians tried to cross in pursuit of them, God stopped the wind that was separating the sea and brought it crashing down upon them. Not one of them survived.

So what changed things? Why was God moved to free the slaves? Why did He stop the Egyptians who pursued them? Because of prayer. The Bible said that God heard the cries of His people and He was moved to deliver them (Exod. 3:7–10). So He did. Prayer moves the heart of God, and He will do incredible, miraculous, unimaginable things to see His children freed from slavery—both physical and spiritual.

## OUR ROLE IN ENDING SLAVERY

God isn't the only component to this story though. Man is part of it. God didn't enslave those people in Egypt, and He didn't enslave the twenty-seven plus million people in slavery today. Man did. And just as it was man who walked in the will of God to set the Hebrews free, it is our job to see those bound by slavery set free.

The Bible says that Jesus came to set the captives free. When we accept Christ and experience this spiritual freedom, it is our duty to see that others bound in the same captivity are set free as well. We are called to share and see people set free not only from spiritual slavery but physical slavery as well.

The work of God and Moses in Exodus was what some would call supernatural. God clearly intervened to help it happen. But what if God doesn't show up in a burning bush and tell you to free some slaves? What if He doesn't give you an anointed staff and send a bunch of plagues, as He did for Moses, to bolster your cause? Should you still act?

YES!

There is a book in the Bible called Philemon. It is one chapter made up of twenty-five verses. It barely takes up half a page.

The Book of Philemon is actually a letter that Paul, the guy we talked about earlier, wrote to his friend Philemon. Philemon owned a slave named Onesimus who ran away. While in prison Paul befriended Onesimus and grew to love him very much. The letter is a plea to Philemon to release and forgive all debts that Onesimus had. In fact, Paul kind of boxes him in a little to do it. The letter actually really makes me laugh. Read some of it below:

> So if you still consider me a comrade-in-arms, welcome him back to you as you would me. If he damaged anything or owes you anything, chalk it up to my account. This is my personal signature—Paul— and I stand behind it. (I don't need to remind you, do I, that you owe your very life to me?) Do me this big favor, friend. You'll be doing it for Christ, but it will also do my heart good. I know you well enough to know you will. You'll probably go far beyond what I've written.
> —PHILEMON 1:17–21, THE MESSAGE

Paul, though he had no obligation to Onesimus at all, wrote on behalf of the runaway slave. We are called to do the same. We have no obligation to see others freed from slavery, but the fact that it moves the heart of God and makes Him happy to see His children free is cause enough.

In 2007, while walking through an airport in Greece, Christine Caine saw handmade posters and pictures everywhere of young women who had gone missing. When she expressed her concern and confusion over how many young women could be missing, it was brought to her attention that they were victims of human trafficking. At first she didn't believe that was the case.[12]

However, in doing her own research, she opened up a world that she had no idea existed. She learned about the practice of young girls being placed on auction blocks and sold to the highest bidder, similar to live-stock. She learned about women who get pregnant in Greek brothels who are then smuggled to Bulgaria to give birth, where their babies are then sold into pedophile rings. She learned about women and girls as young as six who were being drugged and kidnapped from airports and bus stations and sold into sexual slavery all across the world, never to see or speak to their families again.[13]

While anyone else might have seen the enormity of the situation and thought, "I am just one person. What can I do?," Christine thought, "I am one person, and I must do something." In 2008 Christine Caine formed the A21 Campaign. Because of one woman's heart and action thousands and thousands of people have been rescued and rehabilitated from slavery.

We must take the example of women and men such as Christine Caine and Paul, people who know that they can make a difference, that God can use them. We too can make a difference in slavery in the world if we will only be so bold as to say, "I can and I will stand against this."

## OUR HOPE

The world says that our hope in the midst of slavery should be the justice system. They tell us to trust the cops and city officials who are taking care of this problem. The world says, "Why even have hope if every time one girl is rescued, three more are enslaved?" The world says that our hope should be in relief and rescue organizations that will go to the front lines and break down doors.

Our hope in the midst of slavery is this: God has gone to greater lengths to stop slavery than we ever could, and if we will allow Him to, He will continue. While we were yet sinners, bound in spiritual slavery, He sent His Son to die and pay for our freedom, though it was not a debt of His own. He loves us so much that He hears our pleas for freedom and moves on our behalf. He has placed a call on the lives of men and women, some of whom may even be reading this book, who will be as Moses and Christine Caine, who will be frontline soldiers, who will walk into dark places and carry light and freedom with them. For those of us who cannot be frontline soldiers in this battle, He has put within us the ability to pray and see miraculous change because of our prayers.

*Father God, I thank You that You bought my freedom before I ever knew I needed it.*

*I pray right now in Jesus's name for each and every person living in spiritual or physical slavery. I pray that You would touch them and give them peace. I pray that You would send men and women to help free them. I pray You would bring justice to those who cause this pain.*

*Help me never get so focused on myself that I fail to see the world outside of me. Deliver me from spiritual slavery. I rebuke the enemy and his plan to keep me bound in darkness. Help me live free in light.*

*In Jesus's name, amen.*

# 6

# HOPE IN GENOCIDE

*Radical killers empty gun clips in clubs,
Hopeless young mothers drown their kids in bathtubs.*

AVE YOU EVER thought about something so hard and worked yourself up so much that you threw up? You may not be crying or anything; it's as if your brain gets so overwhelmed that it decides to make space by emptying your stomach.

On the night before the first day of school my mom stayed up with me while I threw up. This happened every single year from second grade until the year I graduated high school. Don't ask me why; I have no idea. But you can ask my mom. She will probably laugh now, though we didn't laugh then. She was a single parent with a full-time job, and my brother had to be ready for school the next day too. Still she stayed up with me each time and held my hair while nerves forced me to puke my guts up. Even if I didn't *feel* nervous about school the next day, I still thought and thought about it until I worked myself up so much that I made myself physically ill. It's been a long time since I had a first day of school, but today, for the first time since then, I thought about something so hard it made me sick: this chapter.

I feel book writing etiquette probably says you shouldn't talk about throwing up. It also probably says you shouldn't say things that make you seem like less of an authority on a subject, but I'm about to do that too. The truth is I don't understand why God had me write this book. I am young, less experienced than some, and still on my own faith journey. He picked me anyway, so I'm going to share my heart—both the pain I feel and the hope that can be found.

The idea of wrapping my mind around genocide made me physically sick to my stomach, and once again I started a chapter with a tear-soaked shirt. How do you point people toward hope when they watched as every person they loved was brutally killed and stacked in a pile, as if they were yesterday's trash? How do you explain the goodness and hope of God to someone whose brother went out with friends to Pulse nightclub and never came home? How do you do it?

Acts of genocide are dark, disgusting acts of the enemy that I can hardly fathom. I will never be able to articulate the feeling that I felt in my heart as I researched this topic and saw black-and-white photos of bodies piled so high they looked like small sticks and color photos so bright with blood that I couldn't tell where clothes ended and blood began. I saw photos of children in lines walking into buildings they would never walk out of. I read articles of Armenian women who were forced to walk into the desert in death marches carrying their children at their sides, leaving their husbands behind. I saw stories about Bosnian men beheaded in the center of town while their families watched and wept.

And here I am, safe at my table, trying to figure out how to make sense of any of it myself, let alone how to share hope in the midst of it.

But hope exists, even in our lack of understanding.

## GENOCIDE STARTS WITH A SINGLE THOUGHT

I will never understand genocide. I will never be able to put myself in the shoes of a leader who rationalizes such darkness. I do, however, understand the enemy who causes it. Satan is very real and very angry. He hates God and he hates people. It is literally the mission of his existence to destroy people at all costs. Genocide is one way that he does that. That said, I don't believe he just tells someone to go out and murder a million people. Instead he starts with a small idea planted in someone's head that grows into a seed of bitterness and hate.

In October of 1907 a young man with tremendous skill and a passion for art and drawing withdrew his inheritance from his bank and moved to Vienna, Austria, with hopes of attending one of the most prestigious art schools of his time, the Vienna Academy of Fine Arts. He left behind his mother, who was dying of breast cancer, to pursue the only dream he had ever had. He spent two days doing the entrance exam, fully expecting to get in. While the panel agreed that he was skilled at architecture, he did not show enough promise in appreciation for the human body as an art form.[1]

He spent the next year painting postcards and selling

them to make ends meet until it was time to apply again, only to be rejected a second time in 1908. Though the school was open about why he was rejected and the board spoke to him in detail about why they had not accepted him, this young man was convinced that a Jewish professor had it out for him, and that was why he was never allowed in.[2] That simple thought shaped the ideology that would claim the lives of six million Jewish men, women, and children, as well as millions from other people groups. The young artist's name was Adolf Hitler.

It was a single idea spurring from the simple feeling of rejection that the enemy used to set the wheels of the Holocaust in motion. Satan didn't speak to Adolf Hitler and tell him to murder an entire people group, but he used an idea to grow a seed of hate within Hitler's heart that made it easy for him blame his trouble and the troubles of his country on innocent people.

More often than not, at least in my research, every act of genocide began this way. From Armenia to Bosnia, Germany to Rwanda, it was an idea brought on by a life experience that shaped the men and women who would raise up armies to try to eradicate entire people groups based on their religion, race, gender, color, lifestyle, or nationality. It has been happening since the beginning of time.

## He's Genocide of the Jews

Look at Herod. He is yet another example of a simple idea leading to enough hatred to destroy a group of

people. Herod committed genocide just to try and protect his kingship from a baby.

After Jesus's birth the news of the newly born "king
of the Jews" spread quickly across Jerusalem.

> Now after Jesus was born in Bethlehem of Judea in
> the days of Herod the king, behold, wise men from
> the east came to Jerusalem, saying, "Where is he
> who has been born king of the Jews? For we saw
> his star when it rose and have come to worship him."
> When Herod the king heard this, he was troubled,
> and all Jerusalem with him; and assembling all the
> chief priests and scribes of the people, he inquired
> of them where the Christ was to be born. They told
> him, "In Bethlehem of Judea, for so it is written by
> the prophet: 'And you, O Bethlehem, in the land
> of Judah, are by no means least among the rulers
> of Judah; for from you shall come a ruler who will
> shepherd my people Israel.'"
>
> —MATTHEW 2:1–6

Naturally this prophecy freaked Herod out. The
prophecy said a ruler would be born in Bethlehem, and
here was a young man born in Bethlehem who was
being called the king of the Jews even at birth. Herod,
in fearing for his kingship, decided that something
must be done. So he decided to kill Jesus.

> Then Herod summoned the wise men secretly and
> ascertained from them what time the star had
> appeared. And he sent them to Bethlehem, saying,
> "Go and search diligently for the child, and when
> you have found him, bring me word, that I too may

come and worship him." After listening to the king, they went on their way. And behold, the star that they had seen when it rose went before them until it came to rest over the place where the child was. When they saw the star, they rejoiced exceedingly with great joy. And going into the house they saw the child with Mary his mother, and they fell down and worshiped him. Then, opening their treasures, they offered him gifts, gold and frankincense and myrrh. And being warned in a dream not to return to Herod, they departed to their own country by another way.

—Matthew 2:7–12

As you can imagine, Herod was really mad that the scholars gave him the runaround. Without them he had no way of finding Jesus. Finding out that he had been duped led Herod to commit what is now termed in history as the Massacre of Innocents.

Then Herod, when he saw that he had been tricked by the wise men, became furious, and he sent and killed all the male children in Bethlehem and in all that region who were two years old or under.

—Matthew 2:16

It was the simple idea that Herod would lose his seat as king that caused him to call for the mass murder of every baby boy younger than two. All it took was one thought—a single fear—and something within Herod changed, causing him to do the unthinkable. Not a single one of those children posed a threat to him, and because he didn't even end up killing Jesus in the slaughter, it made their deaths even more needless and absurd.

## CHANGING GENOCIDE BEGINS WITH ME AND WITH YOU

More difficult even than why genocide occurs is the struggle to understand how we change it. How do you change what you cannot understand? I spent a lot of time on this. I thought about it, researched it, prayed about it, cried about it, and prayed about it even more, and finally God spoke to me.

"Savanna, if you want to change environments that breed acts of genocide, you must see it for what it is— the destruction of humanity. In order to combat destruction, something new must be built. You must see value in people, sympathize with them, love them, and build them up. Put the perspective of what it means to be human back where it belongs on both sides—for the victims and the abusers."

I wish you could have seen my face. You know the emoji with the two wide eyes and straight mouth? I was that emoji. I was thinking, "Umm, excuse me, Lord, but that sounds like you're wanting me to feel just as bad for the abusers as I do the victims. They were horrible. I don't know if I can do that."

His reply after that sent me reeling right out of my seat into a heap of tears on the ground: "I was a victim, and I took the cross for my abuser—you."

Cue the face that looks like the weeping emoji.

He was right. It was my sin that sent Him to the cross. He saw me as human and treated me as valuable even though my sins hung Him where He died. He saw me through love-filled lenses, and if I want to stop acts of violence such as these, I too must view people—all people, not just the hurting but those who cause the hurt—through the same love-filled lenses.

The thing is, Jesus loved Hitler and Herod just as much as He loves me. My sins held Him to that cross just as theirs did. That is a hard pill to swallow, you guys, especially after looking at all of those photos. But it is a pill that I must swallow and a truth that I must accept.

Acts of genocide are made possible by taking away the humanity from a group of people and reducing them to the sum of their parts. As unpopular as the idea is, if we are going to fight genocide, we must put humanity back in focus. It is easy for us to judge dictators and men and women who commit atrocities such as genocide. We see them as heartless, vile, dark people who know no love and have no regard for humanity. In many ways those things are true. But the truth of the matter is that we cannot hate those who commit acts of genocide for failing to see the value in humanity when we look at them and in our hurt refuse to acknowledge their humanity as well.

When it boils down to it, we are not so unlike them. Similar to us, these abusers had dreams and goals and intentions. How many times have we known hurt and rejection at the hands of one person and subsequently passed judgment on an entire group of people because of it? It only takes one thought such as "I can't stand people like *that*," "*Those* people abuse the system," or

"*They* get away with everything." Over time such ideas can easily jump from offense to prejudice to genocide. The only difference between a dictator who commits genocide and me is the way that I respond to the things that happen to me.

I don't think any leader who commits genocide dreamed as a ten-year-old they would one day grow up and commit mass murder. It is a slow, painful, dark evolution over time. It is a choice that comes after many hurts.

Hitler was once a boy. He had a family. He was not unlike my own sons. He fell and scraped his knees and needed kisses; he went out with friends and played with toys. He had bad dreams and needed six hundred glasses of water at night, as does every other five-year-old kid that has ever existed. He wanted to be an artist, the same as you when you were little. He was once a four-year-old boy learning to ride a bike, just like you.

That hurts a bit, doesn't it? Making him human, comparing him to us.

If you need to put the book down here and rest awhile and think on this, I understand. It is challenging. It is thought provoking and hard. It was such a difficult idea for me to grasp that I too had to walk away from my computer and ruminate on it in my heart and mind. No hard feelings, friend. I want this book to be challenging, but not angering or burdensome. Find the truth, think it over, and continue—don't just slam the book shut in anger and refusal and never pick it up again. You would be truly missing out on a powerful thought.

Don't get me wrong; I am not saying the acts of

genocide carried out by these men and women are not despicable. They are awful, and I am not making excuses for them. As much as it would make me look like a super Christian to say otherwise, if I were to ever come face-to-face with one of these individuals, he would probably meet something much more intense than a handshake or a hug. And it would probably come in the form of a fist to the face—just being honest.

The point that God was trying to make to me is that we must put on the same lenses of love that He looks at us through when we view them. Where there is no love, there is no hope. We must find a way to love the unlovable in order to bring hope and healing to the hurting.

## SURVIVING AND THRIVING

Rwanda has always had a tumultuous history. Ethnic tensions and shifting political blame caused continual unrest in the country, but in April 1994, when President Juvenal Habyarimana's plane was shot down after taking off, it became the straw that broke the camel's back, and what little peace that existed was destroyed.[3]

> **TWEET ABOUT IT!**
>
> There is no hope without love. We must find a way to love the unlovable in order to bring hope and healing to the hurting. #FIERCEHOPE

Though it is still unclear who caused the attack on the president, the ramifications throughout the country were far reaching. The tension between the Tutsis and

Hutus had been building for some time, so when the president, a Hutu, was killed, the blame was placed on the Tutsi people—though many people believe it was actually the act of Hutu extremists. Almost immediately a plan for retribution was started by Hutu-led government, and the slaughter of the Tutsis and the Hutus who supported them began.[4]

Over a one-hundred-day period innocent men, women, and children, for no other reason than being Tutsi, were murdered. They were drowned, burned, or hanged, or they experienced a different type of gruesome death—one of the many that I don't even want to type out. In the end more than eight hundred thousand people were killed.[5]

During the slaughter a Tutsi woman named Immaculee Ilibagiza went into hiding with seven other women to avoid death. She spent ninety-one of the one-hundred-day genocide huddled together with them in a local pastor's bathroom. She went into the bathroom a healthy, young college student and left the bathroom weighing just sixty-five pounds. She fought to survive, only to find that most everyone she knew, including her entire family, had been murdered.[6]

When asked how she survived, she gives credit to prayer. She speaks openly about how bitterness and anger were destroying her faith and her hope, so she prayed and asked God to work in her heart. He not only answered her prayer, but also later, when she had the opportunity to come face-to-face with the man who killed her mother and her brother, she was able to offer him her unconditional forgiveness.[7]

Immaculee did not let her circumstances define her faith or her future. She found God deeper than ever because she understood that even if God did not intervene in her troubles, it didn't mean that He abandoned her in them. She trusted the plan that He had for her life despite the enemy's attack that nearly ended it. She experienced a side of God that is sometimes only experienced in times of great tragedy.

The Bible says in Isaiah 40:31: "They who wait for the LORD shall renew their strength; they shall mount up with wings like eagles; they shall run and not be weary; they shall walk and not faint." You see, what Immaculee experienced was something that only comes from resilience. It comes from pushing and not giving up. She experienced strength in a way that only comes when you can do nothing but wait on God. In her waiting she found not only strength unimaginable and peace above understanding but also a much greater treasure. God cultivated in her the ability to see her abusers through love-filled lenses, the ability to forgive them.

## FINDING HOPE THROUGH FORGIVENESS

Truth be told, I wanted to give up writing this book more than once. It was hard and it hurt, but the stories of these survivors were part of what kept me going. I read many stories from survivors of all kinds of genocide. I read so many, in fact, that I could fill an entire book with them as opposed to a single chapter. Boy, would that be a book worth reading! These stories are so moving. There is nothing as strong or as empowering as the resiliency of the human spirit, the strength and determination of people to live in the midst of incredible pain, or the power to fight through and survive all odds.

Reading about people who had peace that far surpassed any rational understanding and strength that was only bolstered by their circumstances inspired me to continue. I spent hours reading stories of men, women, and children who lived with the idea that "If I must die, I'll die, but I will not let go of the things that make me who I am." The God-built ability to thrive under pressure and not be crushed in torment shone through some of their stories in ways that I could never even begin to articulate. Anytime I felt so down that I couldn't imagine continuing, I read more survivor stories and once again was bolstered to continue.

It was actually within their stories that I found hope in genocide. There was a trend in the stories of survivors. The men and women who came out of genocide to live happy, successful, full lives all had one thing in common: just as Immaculee Ilibagiza did, they all found a way to forgive those who hurt them. The only thing that separated these survivors from others who survived but lived bound by hurt and pain and torment was one thing: forgiveness.

I watched a video of a tiny old lady wearing a blue blazer that all but engulfed her small frame, bending down to hug an old man in a gray shirt and maroon sweater vest. She speaks to him, and near the end of the video his aged, wrinkled hand wraps around the side of her face and pulls her in as he plants a gentle kiss on her cheek.

If you didn't know the context of the video, you would think it was about two old friends reuniting after time apart. Surprisingly that is not the case.

The woman in the video is named Eva Kor. At the time she was an eighty-one-year-old Jewish woman, and she is a survivor of the Holocaust. She survived Auschwitz, one of the deadliest and most dangerous concentration camps in existence at the time. Heartbreakingly she and her twin sister were the only members of her family who survived. Her father, mother, and two older sisters were all murdered in the gas chambers, and Eva and her twin sister, Miriam, did not have it easy. Some even speculate that death in the gas chambers would have been a better fate.[8]

Eva and Miriam were taken as experimental subjects by a Nazi doctor named Josef Mengele and kept in a hospital ward. Eva was injected with at least five needles per day, three days a week, for nearly a year. On more than one occasion they almost killed her. To this day Eva does not know what was in the injections.[9]

The man who embraces her in the video is not a friend, family member, or fellow survivor. He is ninety-four-year-old Oskar Groening, a former SS Nazi sergeant at Auschwitz. They met at his trial, where she testified for him to be prosecuted for his crimes. The embrace, which spurred the documentary *The Girl Who Forgave the Nazis,* came when Eva offered her forgiveness to the man who had a hand in all the torment she experienced.[10]

While Eva wanted all Nazis to be held accountable for their crimes, she said prison wasn't the answer. She said awareness and forgiveness was. She spoke about how the only way to keep that kind of indescribable act from recurring was to talk about it and walk forward in love and forgiveness. While most every other living survivor opposed her, she said she did not offer forgiveness for them or even for Oskar, but for herself.[11]

Forgiveness for Eva was an act of healing and taking back control from those who had tormented her for so long.

## OUR HOPE

The world says that our hope in the midst of genocide is justice. It says we should meet hate with hate. The world says that the dictators and leaders who commit genocide should get everything they have coming to them. The world says that it is OK to view them as monsters rather than men. The world says that since our pain is just, our hurt is too.

Our hope in the midst of genocide is forgiveness. When we experience hurt, we have two choices: walk forward in forgiveness or walk forward in hatred. It is us choosing to walk forward in forgiveness and not allowing hate to root and fester in our hearts that stops acts such as genocide from being birthed from our pain. Had young Hitler chosen to forgive the professor he felt wronged him, would his hatred of Jews festered so long that it produced the Holocaust? If Eva Kor or Immaculee Ilibagiza had not forgiven their abusers, would they be as free and successful, as they are now? Even Christ forgave His murderers as He hung on the cross: "Father, forgive them, for they know not what they do" (Luke 23:34). Forgiveness is the tool through which we develop love-filled lenses. Forgiveness is what puts the humanity back in focus. Our hope is in Christ forgiving us and us forgiving one another.

> *Father God, I pray for every person who is hurting tonight because of an act of genocide. God, I don't understand it and I can't rationalize it, but You can still work in it.*
>
> *I pray right now that You would wrap Your loving arms around them and comfort those experiencing the effects of genocide and mass murder. Give them peace that passes understanding and hope unimaginable. Empower them to forgive their abusers and experience freedom.*
>
> *God, I ask that You give me love-filled lenses to see people through. Help me walk in forgiveness.*
>
> *I rebuke the enemy and his plan to destroy humanity. I will not be a tool he uses to do despicable things. I will love, build up, sympathize with, and see value in all people even if they are different from me. Rid my heart of every hateful thing.*
>
> *In Jesus's name, amen.*

# HOPE IN TERRORISM

*We all stand waiting, breath hitched in our throat,*
*For a bomb in a subway, a plane, or a boat.*

IMAGINE THAT ONE night you decide to take your family into the city to see a brilliant fireworks display on a national holiday. It is summer, so it's warm out and your skin is sticky with sweat, but still you walk palm in palm, holding hands with your wife. After fifteen years together it is still your favorite thing to do. You each carry one of your two children—your wife with your three-year-old son and you with your six-year-old daughter—to the fireworks viewing location. Even though they haven't had dinner yet, you buy both kids an ice cream cone from a street vendor because you can't resist when your little girl says, "Please, Daddy."

You enjoy life in what seems like slow motion for the next half hour. Both of your children squeal loudly with joy at the bright explosions happening out in front of them. Your daughter is perched high atop your shoulders to get the best view, and you're not even upset that you can feel her ice cream dripping onto your neck. You feel too much joy be worried about it, and you don't want to ruin the moment by correcting her. After all, a little sticky mess never hurt anyone.

You look over at your wife and think to yourself that she is more beautiful now than the first time you saw her. She looks back at you and smiles in a way that says she knows what you're thinking and nods that she feels the same way about you. You're just staring at her now, drinking her in. You're thinking about how big your son looks in her arms, and how their smiling profiles are near identical. You remember the fireworks at your wedding and how pretty your wife's white dress looked reflecting the colors of the lights in the sky. She's wearing the little diamond earrings you bought her for your first Christmas together, but you're not surprised because she never takes them off.

You are so enveloped in the memories that you have all but drowned out the sound of fireworks in your ears. A scream rips you back to reality in just enough time to look over your wife's shoulder and see the large white cargo truck on the sidewalk barreling toward your little family of four. You want to scream or push them or react, but the truck is already too close. Before you can even blink, you watch the front of the truck swallow your wife and son just moments before you and your daughter are tangled beneath it with them. Then, nothing. No more memories. Your life and the lives of all you love are no more.

That may be the most upsetting story I have written this whole book. There is no redemptive moment, no point of forgiveness, and no clarity of action. Just death.

But that is not why it is upsetting. It is upsetting because it is not a story at all. It is the harsh reality that hundreds of men, women, and children experienced at a Bastille Day celebration in Nice, France, on July 14, 2016. While thousands of unsuspecting friends and families enjoyed a fireworks display at the Promenade des Anglais that Thursday evening, an Islamic extremist and member of ISIS named Mohamed Lahouaiej-Bouhlel got behind the wheel of a nineteen-ton cargo truck and deliberately drove it as fast as he could into the crowd of onlookers. He drove the truck in an intentional zigzag motion on and off the sidewalk to hit as many people as he could.[1] In the five minutes between when he started the drive and when he was killed by police in an exchange of gunfire, he injured more than two hundred people and claimed the lives of eighty-five, ten of whom were children and teenagers.[2]

The terrorist attack in Nice came just one month after Omar Mateen opened fire in Pulse, an Orlando night-club, killing forty-nine people and injuring fifty-three more. In what has been dubbed the deadliest shooting by a single shooter in US history, Mateen walked into Pulse and fired 110 rounds into the crowd of men and women who were inside—unprovoked and unassisted. He carried out the worst terrorist attack on US soil since 9/11 in the name of the Islamic State.[3]

## TWISTED IDEALS LEAD TO TERRORISM

It was the Pulse shooting that prompted the posting of the spoken word that this book is written around. There were many other major terrorist attacks and countless minor ones that occurred in the four-week time span between the Pulse shooting in Orlando and the Bastille Day attack in Nice. In fact, only six months into 2016 the year was already being dubbed and remembered as the year that terrorist attacks happened nearly every day all throughout the world.[4] Each day various members of radical religions and political extremist groups commit heinous crimes against humanity.

Whether it is flying a plane into a major city sky-scraper, driving a car into a crowded coffee shop, or simply a person with a bomb strapped on running into the middle of a crowded airport, these men, women, and sadly even children are doing what they believe is the best course of action in order to see their twisted ideals recognized.

And this is the part where I will make many people upset, but it must be said, so stick with me. Though radical Islamic terrorists do commit such acts, they are not the only ones. No one religion or organization has the monopoly on terrorism. I won't pretend or turn a blind eye to the fact that there have also been members of other radical religious organizations, including radical Christian groups, that have committed both domestic and international terrorism.

Blind eyes and silent mouths don't fix broken systems. It is the same hate and warped religious views that cause Islamic extremist suicide bombers to run into crowded bus stations and Westboro Baptist Church to boycott American soldiers. As a pastor and someone with an intimate relationship with Christ, it is enraging and heartbreaking to hear of anyone committing an act of terror in the name of God.

Jesus was the personification (a fancy word for *physical form and representation*) of God, and relationship with God is made possible through, and only through, Christ's work on the cross. Regardless of what anyone says, religion based on a works mentality, especially radical religion, is the perversion of who God is and how to please Him. As long as people continue to allow the enemy to breed hate in their hearts, terrorism will continue to exist—no matter what organization's name we slap on it.

Remember, it is the enemy's goal to keep us separated from God. That is how this whole story began. He knows that when we are connected to God and in communion with God, we are an unstoppable force for good in the world. In order to separate us from God, he will deceive man and skew the perspective of what it takes to be in relationship with God. It only takes one distorted perspective to throw an entire good-intentioned, well-meaning person off balance.

---

### TWEET ABOUT IT!

Radical religion is the perversion of who God is and how to please Him. #FIERCEHOPE

---

## SAUL OF TARSUS, A NEW TESTAMENT TERRORIST

Throwing off that balance and leading people to commit terroristic acts is something the enemy has been working at for years. Obviously the technology did not exist in Jesus's day for terrorist attacks using gunfire, plane crashes, or car bombs, but terrorists did exist. In fact, if one such terrorist didn't exist, we wouldn't have half of the New Testament.

Saul of Tarsus was a well-educated, financially secure, devout Jewish man and Roman citizen. He was among the elite. Just as his father before him, he was a Pharisee (meaning he was a self-righteous religious dude bound by a bunch of hard-core laws) who received his education in religion, philosophy, ethics, literature, and more from one of the greatest rabbis in history—a man named Gamaliel, who was a doctor of Jewish law (Acts 5:34; 22:3; 23:6). Think about if the dean of Harvard Law School taught you all of your lessons one-on-one; that is the kind of education Saul received. Because Saul received such a strict Jewish education and because his father was also a Pharisee, Saul made it his mission to see to it that everyone adhered to the Jewish religion, or at least the version of the Jewish religion that Saul felt was correct.

This is what Saul says about himself in the Bible:

> You know my pedigree: a legitimate birth, circumcised on the eighth day; an Israelite from the elite tribe of Benjamin; a strict and devout adherent to God's law; a fiery defender of the purity of my religion, even to the point of persecuting the church; a meticulous observer of everything set down in God's law Book.
>
> —PHILIPPIANS 3:4–6, THE MESSAGE

You're probably thinking all is well and good. I mean, he sounds as if he was a rich, smart, passionate Jewish fellow, and you'd be right. He was those things. But there is a second component to that verse. It was not until Saul took it upon himself to become a "fiery defender of the purity" of his religion that things start to get a little skewed (Phil. 3:6, THE MESSAGE). It is in that sentence that Saul of Tarsus becomes just like the men and women we talked about above who committed acts of terrorism they justified with warped perspectives of religious ideals. Everything Paul believed, even the God he believed in, was real and correct. But when he became so bound by law and his own ideas about how that law should be practiced, Saul's view of who God was and what He would look like when He appeared was skewed. Saul had only known religion, so when relationship presented itself, he did not recognize it. He punished those who did recognize it.

Here is a quick little side note to give you some context: it was the Pharisees who killed Jesus. Pretty crazy, right? The men who spent their lives learning about Jewish customs and God's law killed the very man they believed would come to deliver them. When Jesus burst on the scene, He didn't look or act like what the Pharisees believed the true Messiah would. Pharisees were considered the highest of the high in society, and Jesus didn't act like that at all. He hung out with low-lifes, He partied at weddings, He touched sick people, He made bold declarations, and He had a lack of respect for their religious traditions. Not only was He the complete opposite of a Pharisee, but He was also a threat to their entire elitist system. They had spent their lives adhering to strict laws, so they naturally believed that the Son of God would do the same. When He didn't, instead of adjusting their perspectives to fit the person of Jesus and beginning relationship with Him, the Pharisees kept their religious perspectives, called Jesus blasphemous (just a word for saying Jesus had disrespectful words and actions relating to God), and sentenced Him to death.

OK, back to Saul. After Jesus died and rose again, the Christian movement began to spread quickly. Saul was not a fan of this. He hated Christians because they believed in a version of the Messiah that was different than the one he believed in. Saul made it his mission to capture, accuse, and imprison or execute any Christian who believed in or openly professed Jesus as Lord.

Saul's action against Christians started with a man named Stephen. The Bible called Stephen a young man full of faith and the Holy Spirit. He was traveling with some other disciples just spreading the gospel:

> And the word of God continued to increase, and the number of the disciples multiplied greatly in Jerusalem, and a great many of the priests became obedient to the faith. And Stephen, full of grace and power, was doing great wonders and signs among the people. Then some of those who belonged to the synagogue of the Freedmen (as it was called), and of the Cyrenians, and of the Alexandrians, and of those from Cilicia and Asia, rose up and disputed

with Stephen. But they could not withstand the wisdom and the Spirit with which he was speaking.

—Acts 6:7–10

As it says, men argued with Stephen, but the men and their arguments were no match for Stephen and his wisdom and spirit. So, like any hearty bunch of angry sore losers, they went and lied to some religious leaders in the city and said they heard Stephen cursing God. Stephen was brought before the high council, and he could easily have brought witnesses to vindicate himself. Instead he took the opportunity to preach to the very men who accused him. I wish I could say that their hearts were moved and they changed their minds, but they didn't. A mob formed and stoned Stephen until he died.

The Bible says that Saul not only watched and approved of Stephen's death, but also that he even held the coats of the men who stoned him. Saul's participation in the death of Stephen set a chain of events in motion that would forever alter the course of his life:

> And Saul approved of his execution. And there arose on that day a great persecution against the church in Jerusalem.... But Saul was ravaging the church, and entering house after house, he dragged off men and women and committed them to prison.
>
> —Acts 8:1, 3

> But Saul, still breathing threats and murder against the disciples of the Lord, went to the high priest and asked him for letters to the synagogues at Damascus, so that if he found any belonging to the

Way, men or women, he might bring them bound
to Jerusalem.

—Acts 9:1–2

Saul went on a rampage against Christians. In many
ways his persecution and murder of Christians can be
compared to that of radical religious terrorism today.
Every death or imprisonment that Saul called for or
caused himself was birthed out of a twisted view of
God and His laws. Saul truly believed that it was what
God would want. His intentions, however warped, were
pure.

However, Saul's pure intentions did not make his acts
of terrorism on the Christian church right or justified
or any less heinous. If it was Saul's skewed view of God
that started that mess, it would take that view being
adjusted to stop it. That is exactly what happened.

## CHANGING SAUL

Saul was going to Damascus one day, and the Bible
says that a blinding light dazed him and he fell to the
ground. While on the ground, he heard a voice speak
to him:

> And falling to the ground he heard a voice saying
> to him, "Saul, Saul, why are you persecuting me?"
> And he said, "Who are you, Lord?" And he said, "I
> am Jesus, whom you are persecuting."
>
> —Acts 9:4–5

I feel that if ever there was a moment when wetting
yourself was justified, it would be this moment, when

you're heading to kill Christians because they follow Jesus and Jesus shows up and asks you why you're doing it.

Saul didn't wet himself, but he did lose his dignity. When he stood up, Saul realized that he had lost his sight and was completely blind. Saul, the man whose very sight struck terror into the hearts of those who saw him enter a city, had to be led by hand, as if he were a child, into Damascus, and he remained blind for three days.

In Damascus there was a disciple named Ananias. The Lord spoke to him in a vision and told him to go to where Saul was and lay hands on him to help him regain his sight. As you can imagine, Ananias knew who Saul was and wasn't so jazzed about the idea.

> But Ananias answered, "Lord, I have heard from many about this man, how much evil he has done to your saints at Jerusalem. And here he has authority from the chief priests to bind all who call on your name."
>
> —Acts 9:13–14

But the Lord had a plan for Saul:

> But the Lord said to him, "Go, for he is a chosen instrument of mine to carry my name before the Gentiles and kings and the children of Israel. For I will show him how much he must suffer for the sake of my name."
>
> —Acts 9:15–16

Ananias listened and got up and went. I mean, when the Lord says go, you go. So Ananias headed to where Saul was and laid hands on him and prayed for him. And just as God said, Saul gained back his sight. Then Saul got baptized and ate some food (he obviously had his priorities together), and his body was strengthened.

If the story ended here, it would be a good story. Saul was changed; he was no longer going to kill Christians. In fact, he became a Christian himself, and the lives of countless men and women were spared. But the story doesn't end there. This isn't just a good story; it's a great one.

In case you haven't figured it out by now, when Saul did something, he did it hard. When he was a Pharisee, he was 100 percent *sold out*—so sold out that he basically became a terrorist. So it is no surprise that when he experienced a life change to the other extreme, he sold out again. He was all in: he dove in headfirst. There was no toe dipping, water testing, or weenie baby jumping in. He went just as hard as he had before.

> For some days he was with the disciples at Damascus. And immediately he proclaimed Jesus in the synagogues, saying, "He is the Son of God."
>
> —ACTS 9:19–20

---

### TWEET ABOUT IT!

Religion sets us up for failure; relationship sets us up for freedom. #FIERCEHOPE

---

After that, Saul did not stop spreading the gospel until his death. He was stoned, beaten, imprisoned, and chased out of cities for the rest of his life. Saul went on to become one of the greatest apostles and theologians ever to exist. He was responsible for more conversions, trained disciples, and church plants than any other individual in the Bible. He even penned about half of the entire New Testament. To this day the modern church still applies his leadership styles and teachings on topics ranging from parenting and marriage to salvation and correction. His contribution to the Christian church will forever reverberate through history. Wondering why you've never heard of him? Because you probably know him by his Roman name—Paul.

## TURNING TERRORIST SAUL INTO APOSTLE PAUL

So what changed the terrorist Saul into the apostle Paul? Was it a different view of God? Was it a new perspective of religion? Was it a new religion?

No, I believe it was just the opposite of these—it was the abolishment of religion altogether. It was the change in dynamic of what Saul believed in as a result of his encounter with Jesus. He went from believing in a religion *about* a Man to having a relationship *with* that Man. Religion sets us up for failure; relationship sets us up for freedom.

When Jesus appeared to Saul on the road to Damascus that day, He was saying, "Here I am. I am real. I am not who you think I am. Why are you doing this to Me?" Suddenly every preconceived notion that Saul had about God's law and who the Messiah was were

119

shattered. The bright light that blinded Saul on the road that day pierced through the misshapen ideals Saul had. Though he lost his sight, for the first time in a long time Saul had clarity.

It is such a beautiful thought that Saul was never too far gone for God to reach him. The Bible says that Saul was chosen by God to be a carrier of His name, even though Saul spent his days betraying that name. If God could encounter a radical religious zealot who was killing and imprisoning the very people God loved most and change his life on a rocky dirt road, I can believe and hope that God can encounter a radical religious zealot who plans to strap on a bomb to his chest and run into a bazaar full of people and change his life too.

---

**TWEET ABOUT IT!**

No heart is ever too hard, no hurt ever too deep, and no life ever too far gone that God cannot reach it. **#FIERCEHOPE**

---

## RELIGION VS. RELATIONSHIP

Our hope in the midst of terrorism is not religion; it's in relationship—relationship with God and relationship with each other.

Religion doesn't end wars; it starts them. Relationship says, "I love you too much and know you too well to go to war with you or over you."

Religion doesn't fix problems; it creates them.

Relationship says, "There is no problem too big that I cannot fix."

Religion doesn't cure hurt; it causes it. Relationship says, "I will bring healing to your old wounds and protect you from new ones."

Religion doesn't free us from standards; it shackles us with them. Relationship says, "I was perfect so you don't have to be."

Religion doesn't absolve us of sin; it demands payment for it. Relationship says, "I did it so you don't have to."

I believe that the last thing God wants is someone climbing behind the wheel of a cargo truck and driving into a crowded group of people and shouting "God is greatest!" I believe that the last thing God wants is someone walking into an abortion clinic, taking hostages, and opening fire in the name of saving babies for Him. I believe that the last thing God wants is a young man to walk into a church and gun down the men and women who peacefully pray there in hope of starting a war.

More than anything I believe that God is tired of people slapping His name on a label of approval across their bad decisions.

These radical, religion-wielding terrorists live with a view of God that the enemy has so distorted and corrupted that He no longer looks like the merciful father who longs to be close, but instead like a slave-driving tyrant who can be won over with works.

Perhaps if these terrorists had a relationship with Jesus, they would know His heart, and they would know that you can't buy your way into heaven with a bomb. If they talked to God and listened to what He has to say, they would know that He loves the sinner and the saint equally and He gets no joy in His lost children being gunned down. If they spent time in His presence, they would know that He is tender and loving and good.

## OUR HOPE

The world says that the hope in the midst of terrorism is weapons. The world tells us to put our hope and faith in the armed forces of the government to go in, crash, and smash all enemies, both foreign and domestic. The world tells us that our hope lies in our ability to put stricter guidelines and parameters on religions and limit how and why they do things. The world says that we should put our hope in the Department of Defense and its ability to protect us.

Our hope in the midst of terrorism is relationship—with God and with others. God is not an ethereal figure that we develop dogmas about; He is a person who wants to be known by you. He wants more than to merely be believed in. We believe in laws of nature and forces of wind that we cannot see, but we have no affection for them; we do not speak to them about our circumstances or embrace them with our words of love. He doesn't want only to be believed. He wants to be experienced. He wants to be a daily part of your lives. He describes Himself in the Bible as a friend, a husband, and a father—all deeply personal, relational terms.

God's love for us and our acceptance by Him are not predicated on reaching a certain religious standard.

They are freely given and made possible by Jesus and His work on the cross. Our relationship with God cannot be bought or bolstered by completing a checklist of activities and behaviors.

We also need to pursue right relationship with one another. In the same way as our relationship with God, we must not approach our relationships with one another as a checklist either. We must love freely, and we must ferociously combat hate. No one is ever too bad or too far gone to be reached. We must love them first, as we ourselves were first loved by God.

Fierce hope will never be found in a religion; it will be found only in relationship.

> *Father God, right now I pray for every single victim of an act of terrorism. I pray that You would bring peace, healing, and wholeness to them. God, only You can fix that kind of brokenness.*
>
> *I pray for every religious extremist who intends to commit an act of terror from this point forward. Change their hearts. Restore the broken perspectives the enemy has given them.*
>
> *I thank You for relationship instead of religion. I thank You that religion was nailed to the cross when You were.*
>
> *Thank You for making this all about You and not about me. I am not good enough—I will never be good enough—but You are good enough for both of us.*

*Kill in me any religious spirit that may exist, no matter how pure my intentions are. Help me walk in relationship with You.*

*In Jesus's name, amen.*

# 8

# HOPE IN WAR

Soldiers lay down their lives in Middle Eastern
war zones.
They leave for deployment and never come home.

THE UNITED STATES has used war as such a form
of entertainment that unless we are directly affected
by it, we are oblivious to what it is really like. We
take battle scenes from *American Sniper* and fuse them
together with maps and weapons from *Call of Duty*, and
then we convince ourselves that because we know what
a grenade does and can pronounce the word *Fallujah*,
we know something about war.

I know I did. I took what I read in books, saw in
movies, and played in games and built an Americanized
entertainment-turned-reality version of what I believed
war was like. I feel I am not alone in that.

Apart from the servicemen and servicewomen who
have been directly affected by war, I think most civilian
Americans are spoiled, and we take for granted the cost
that men and women, sons and daughters, and wives
and husbands have paid to keep us spoiled. The truth

is the majority of us have never been pushed out of our cities by foreign military, our government buildings don't get hit by air raids, and our houses don't have fully stocked underground bunkers or bomb shelters. (That is, unless you have been on the show *Doomsday Preppers*. If that is you, just know that I am coming to your house if things ever go south.) We haven't felt the effects of war on mainland American soil in a long time—not since World War II, in the midforties. That pretty much means that those younger than seventy-one years of age, unless they enlisted and did a tour of duty, have not seen the life-altering, world-shattering, mind-numbing reality of war.

Before you get all enraged and stomp off to your computer to get Amazon to refund your money for this book because your son did a tour of duty, before you begin shouting at the pages of this book, "You can't tell me I don't know the effects of war! I had to deal with the idea of losing him every day!," I want you to know that you're right. I can't tell you that. You, as well as any other person reading this book who has hugged a person in the service and waved him off wondering if you would ever see him again, have experienced the effects of war. You know the fear, you know the pain, and you know the loss.

But I also think every man or woman who has ever been deployed into a war zone would agree with me when I say that while we feel the effects of war, we have no idea what those who are living in it go through. We can't comprehend what it's like to fall asleep on a hard cot with the sounds of bombs in the distance. We don't understand how it feels to hold a friend while he bleeds to death from the places that his legs used to be. We haven't ever had to deal with the fact that we are desperate for companionship, but we can't share a bed with anyone because of our night terrors. We've never had to look through the scope of rifle and kill the person on the other end before he killed us, pushing out the thought that he might be someone's husband or son.

We laugh as tears stream down our faces when we see the homecoming videos of parents and their kids on YouTube. We gasp when we watch the flag-draped coffins being unloaded from the backs of planes on the news. We buy our tickets to movies such as *Zero Dark Thirty* and *Lone Survivor* and stand and clap at the end even though the actors and most members of the audience may never know what war really is. When Veterans Day and Memorial Day roll around, we make sure to post a picture we quickly pulled off Google of the American flag or Arlington National Cemetery and hashtag it #heroes before we head off to family get-togethers and festivities. We do those things, and then we convince ourselves that we know something about war.

We don't, you guys. We just don't.

## A Man Who Knows War

But Will does.

Will is my friend, and he recently spent the afternoon at my house, sitting with me on my porch, telling me about the last seven years of his life—seven years that encompassed enlistment, two deployments, and re-adjustment to life outside the military.

Before I talked to Will that day, I had a really clear picture of what this chapter would be. The picture of war that he shared with me was so much different, though. I came prepared with questions, and as we sat across from each other, my pen and steno pad in hand, I asked the first one. I don't know if it was how genuine and open he was or how different his story was from what I imagined, but about a quarter of the way in I switched on the voice recorder on my phone and stopped trying to take notes and just listened to him tell me his story. Two hours later we were finished, and every preconceived notion I had about deployment, soldiers, and life after war was shattered.

Will is a handsome, fit, cultured, intelligent guy. He smiles a lot, he's friendly, helpful, attentive, and kind. He's just not the type of person you picture having any trouble in life. But he did.

Will was nineteen when he enlisted in the Marine Corps. He went to boot camp, and after he finished, he went for specialty training as a mortarman. Then he found out that on his first tour of duty he would be deploying to Afghanistan. Their mission, when they arrived, was to be dropped into a city by helicopter under the cover of darkness and then push the Taliban out. The helicopter lowered and dropped Will and his fellow soldiers into a muddy field. Then the shooting began. They returned fire, and during that four-hour firefight, Will killed someone for the first time. He watched through his scope as the round connected with the Taliban insurgent's chest before he shuttered and fell to the ground. When the firefight ended, they moved to their second location, where an enemy sniper pinned them down for twelve hours. It was during that twelve-hour pin down that he first saw a fellow marine killed.

"I'm just talking to this guy like twenty minutes before, only ever said a word in passing. He's running back and forth, and then I heard the sniper round go off and he dropped on the ground. Then they came out a couple of minutes later and said he was dead," Will said.

Will had always been a Christian. The first memory I have of him is his coming up to the front of the sanctuary in church in uniform so we could pray over him as he headed off for boot camp; this happened again when he was deployed. He accepted Jesus when he was six and was raised in church. Will served in many capacities, but his favorite was serving in the kid's department. He loves kids, and for him the pinnacle of life is a wife and family. It was the experiences he had with kids in Afghanistan that caused him to lose his faith in God.

Will was in a bazaar, which is a shopping area, that was next to a creek the people would frequent to get water. There was an IED there, and it blew up next to an eight-year-old boy and a six-year-old girl. Will said about this experience, "The locals came running over, and they had to pick up what was left of the girl, and then they picked up the boy, who was missing an arm and a leg, and loaded him in a truck and tried to take him to a doctor at our base. But I think the boy ended up dying like...five minutes later."

This wasn't the only instance of kids getting hurt. Later, after Will was hit with an IED and was in the hospital, he woke up after surgery next to a little boy. "He was probably eight years old, and half of his body was burnt. He got burned so bad that his arm was fused to his side. He would just cry all night in his bed, and he kept saying something over and over again, so I asked an interpreter what he was saying. And he told me that the boy was saying he just wanted to die."

For Will it was one thing to see an adult injured, but kids were something else. After these experiences and more of kids being hurt or killed, he lost all faith. Will couldn't understand why, if God was real, He would let things like that happen. Not only that, but he was spending his days fighting Taliban men who were doing all of these heinous acts in the name of religion. In his mind, religion caused the situation he was in, and we would better off without all of it.

It was Will's experience with children during his first deployment that caused him to lose faith, but it was his experience with men during his second deployment that caused him to regain it. Will went on his second deployment as a team leader, meaning he was directly responsible for four guys other than himself, four guys he had to get back home safely to their families. It was the weight of that reality that brought his faith back to him.

During his first deployment Will felt invincible, thinking, "It's never going to be me that gets hurt." But then Will did get wounded when an IED (improvised explosive device) planted by the Taliban blew up next to him. When he was deployed for the second time, he said it felt "much more real for me."

He said, "Not only did I have to worry about me, but I have these guys to worry about. The guys I'm in charge of...the guys whose families I've met, whose mothers I've talked to. This time I knew, I'm not invincible, they're not invincible, and it just brought on a whole bunch of worry. When you see people around you die and you realize how fragile you are and how quickly it can happen, that fear of death starts to creep in. So about half way through my second deployment, before every patrol I would say a prayer and I would just feel much better...you know, like peace. Part of the prayer was, 'Lord, let me make it, but if I die, let it be in such a way that saves my men.' And that took the fear out of me about dying."

It was the reality of death and his responsibility to protect his team from it that pushed Will back into relationship with God. He knew that when it came down to it, he couldn't stop anyone from dying, but he knew the One who could. Will wasn't the only one who felt that way either.

"There was this kid in my platoon who worshipped Satan. Like for real, he claimed he worshipped Satan, and I remember we got in a firefight one time where we were pinned down pretty good and I just remember hearing this guy pray to God and I started to laugh." (This story actually made me laugh really hard. I liked listening to him tell it, because he laughed too.)

For Will it wasn't just the comfort he received in praying, but the experience of supernatural protection that really solidified in him the reestablishment of his faith and his relationship with God. It was in those moments when there was no logical explanation for them to be alive that he had to believe in something greater than himself.

"Then there were times like when you knew you should have died. You could just feel it; this bullet was meant for you, and then suddenly a force would move it—or you—out of the way, and you just knew, I should never have lived through that. You just felt at times so protected."

Even with his faith in God reestablished, Will still struggled transitioning from war zone to civilian life. Will explained to me that in order to survive in high-intensity combat situations, you can't be emotional. The military trains you to turn off that switch in your brain. The problem is that they don't tell you how to turn it back on. He suffered from post-traumatic stress disorder (PTSD), depression, and flashbacks that he self-medicated with alcohol to cope with. Nightmares and being accustomed to sleeping in combat zones and having to wake at the slightest sound made it impossible for him to sleep well. He drank from the time he woke up until he went to bed, even drinking from a flask if he was in college classes that day.

Will lived like this for months. It wasn't until he and his roommate, who also struggled with PTSD and alcoholism, got into a fistfight that triggered a flashback and caused him to black out that he decided to get help. He stopped drinking cold turkey; it took two weeks before he could get out of bed and begin to function again, and then he began therapy.[1]

---

**TWEET ABOUT IT!**

Thank you to the men and women who have given their lives to preserve our right to worship the One who freely gave His. **#FIERCEHOPE**

---

Today Will is a sober, hardworking college student. He is a good friend, and his relationship with God is one of the best places it has ever been in. I am honored to know him, and I was so thankful he let me hear his story. The things he told me completely changed my perspective and opinion on war. I always felt that war was over when you came home, but I learned that sometimes it's when you come home that the real battle begins. I could never imagine fighting in a war and then coming home to fight a new war within yourself.

I want to thank every person who has ever served in the military that might be reading this, especially those who have served in combat zones. Thank you for your sacrifice. I honor you; I deeply honor you. Part of the hope we have in war is the people whom God calls and empowers to boldly fight on the front lines of battle to keep those of us at home safe—people such as Will, who put his life and limbs on the line to protect his country. Thank you to those who have given their lives to preserve our right to worship the One who freely gave His.

## God Is With Us, Even in War

It was Will's stories of feeling that God was with him overseas that encouraged me the most. I read stories and articles from many men and women who believe that God is not with us in war. That really bummed me out, because it's not true, and also because it creates a really bleak outlook on life.

The Bible seems to be a giant book of war from beginning to end. Seriously. The Old Testament deals with physical wars, and the New Testament deals with spiritual ones. I had so much material for this chapter that I could write sixty-six chapters on it. (This a punny—pun + funny = punny—joke.)

One of my favorite war stories in the Bible is about a guy named Gideon. The story of Gideon is not just an example of God being with us in war, but of God empowering the unlikeliest of heroes to win war. The people of Israel were living in an area that was being overpowered by Midianites. One day while Gideon was threshing wheat, in hiding, I might add, because he was a wimpy guy and doesn't want the Midianites to see him, an angel showed up and said, "The LORD is with you, O mighty man of valor" (Judg. 6:12).

And Gideon responded with (and this is a paraphrase), "Umm, how about no, He's not. If He *was*, then He wouldn't be letting these Midianites keep us under their feet. He's turned His back on us, but good try." Then the Bible said the Lord turned and faced him directly. I always read that verse and picture God whipping His head around and saying, "Excuse Me, sir, *but who you talkin' 'bout?*" God didn't do that though.

> And the LORD turned to him and said, "Go in this might of yours and save Israel from the hand of Midian; do not I send you?" And he said to him, "Please, Lord, how can I save Israel? Behold, my clan is the weakest in Manasseh, and I am the least in my father's house." And the LORD said to him, "But I will be with you, and you shall strike the Midianites as one man."
>
> —JUDGES 6:14–16

Gideon was panicking a little at this point. God was calling him to war, and he was the weakest guy in his whole tribe. Not only was he the weakest guy in his tribe, but also his tribe was the weakest tribe in the group of tribes. Five minutes before this Gideon was content to thresh wheat; he wasn't trying to become a soldier. So you can imagine that when God Himself looks him in the face and says, "You, the smallest and weakest, will fight and beat the biggest and strongest, and win," that Gideon was in a bit of disbelief. As if God showing up isn't enough proof, Gideon challenged God to prove it:

> And he said to him, "If now I have found favor in your eyes, then show me a sign that it is you who speak with me. Please do not depart from here until I come to you and bring out my present and set it before you." And he said, "I will stay till you return."
>
> —JUDGES 6:17–18

Gideon went and got a goat and some bread and put it on a rock under the tree where the angel of God was. Gideon poured a bunch of broth over the meat and the bread so they became soppy and wet. The angel of God stretched out the stick he was holding and touched the meat and bread. The entire rock burst into flames and engulfed the meat and bread. The Bible says that Gideon knew then that it was the angel of God. Gideon built an altar for God, blew a ram's horn, and spread the word throughout the area they he needed men to come and report for battle. (See Judges 6:19–35.) Thirty-two thousand men came, but the Midianites had 135,000, so Gideon got cold feet and asked God again to prove that He was calling Gideon to fight this war:

> Then Gideon said to God, "If you will save Israel by my hand, as you have said, behold, I am laying a fleece of wool on the threshing floor. If there is dew on the fleece alone, and it is dry on all the ground, then I shall know that you will save Israel by my hand, as you have said." And it was so. When he rose early next morning and squeezed the fleece, he wrung enough dew from the fleece to fill a bowl with water. Then Gideon said to God, "Let not your anger burn against me; let me speak just once more. Please let me test just once more with the fleece. Please let it be dry on the fleece only, and on all the ground let there be dew." And God did so that night; and it was dry on the fleece only, and on all the ground there was dew.
>
> —JUDGES 6:36–40

Those were signs enough for Gideon. He got up early the next day with his thirty-two thousand troops and set up camp at a spring adjacent to the Midianite camp. Though the Israelites were still outnumbered by more than four times their men, God thought it was still too many for Him to get the credit:

> The LORD said to Gideon, "The people with you are too many for me to give the Midianites into their hand, lest Israel boast over me, saying, 'My own hand has saved me.' Now therefore proclaim in the ears of the people, saying, 'Whoever is fearful and trembling, let him return home and hurry away from Mount Gilead.'" Then 22,000 of the people returned, and 10,000 remained.
>
> —JUDGES 7:2–3

Since 22,000 cowards left, they were down to just 10,000 men. Ten thousand against 135,000 are impossible odds. It seems as if God could definitely get the credit for that win, right? Wrong. God said it was still too many.

> And the LORD said to Gideon, "The people are still too many. Take them down to the water, and I will test them for you there, and anyone of whom I say to you, 'This one shall go with you,' shall go with you, and anyone of whom I say to you, 'This one shall not go with you,' shall not go." So he brought the people down to the water. And the Lord said to Gideon, "Every one who laps the water with his tongue, as a dog laps, you shall set by himself. Likewise, every one who kneels down to drink."

> And the number of those who lapped, putting their hands to their mouths, was 300 men, but all the rest of the people knelt down to drink water. And the LORD said to Gideon, "With the 300 men who lapped I will save you and give the Midianites into your hand, and let all the others go every man to his home."
>
> —JUDGES 7:4–7

I would have some choice words with the Lord. If I worked hard to get thirty-two thousand men and it still looked like a losing battle, and then God tells me to get rid of all but 1 percent of them, I would be upset—really upset. If Gideon thought he might lose before, he was probably really feeling like a dead man walking now. God must have known that, because He came to Gideon and told him that if he would get up and go down to where the Midianite camp was, he could hear what they were saying and he would feel bold and confident once again. While listening, Gideon heard two soldiers talking. One was telling the other about a dream that he had, and the soldier who was listening interpreted the dream as a sign that they would lose the battle to Gideon. Immediately Gideon prayed and thanked God and went to wake up his men.

> And he divided the 300 men into three companies and put trumpets into the hands of all of them and empty jars, with torches inside the jars.
>
> —JUDGES 7:16

He told all of his men that when he gave the signal, they needed to blow their trumpets, smash their jars, and shout, "A sword for the LORD and for Gideon!" (Judg. 7:20). And do you know what happened? The Midianites woke up so confused that they started fighting each other, and those who didn't die at camp and fled were chased after and taken. Gideon and his army of only 300 beat an army that was more than four hundred times bigger than them—because of God.

> ### TWEET ABOUT IT!
> God will raise up people to lead a charge against injustice and imprisonment of His people and will see them through to success.
> **#FIERCEHOPE**

God called an unlikely soldier to rise up and lead an army. He was a weak man in a weak place, but God called courage, strength, vision, and leadership out of him. God equipped him to carry out an enormous task, and all it took was his faithfulness and obedience to the plan and voice of God. God doesn't just need jacked G.I. Joes to get the job done; He also needs regular Joes who will just listen to what He wants them to do.

God never left Gideon. Not when He called him to battle, not when he prepared for battle, and not when he went to battle. God is with us in war, especially when He calls us to it to deliver people who are oppressed, broken, and being kept pinned under their enemy's feet. God will raise up men and women to lead a charge against the injustice, imprisonment, and abuse of His people, and He will see them through to success.

## Seek God in War

There is a second component to war, though. It is easy to say that God is with us when we win, but what about when we lose? Is God with us then? What happens when we locate the enemy but they destroy us before we destroy them? Is it because God abandoned us?

Remember when I said that the entire Bible is a book of war? I personally read about over eighty battles, and those are just the ones documented in Scripture. Want to know something about those battles? The Israelites (God's chosen people) didn't win them all; they lost many too. One such story is the story of Israel, the Philistines, and the ark of the covenant.

Just as He did with Gideon, God would give the Israelites special guidelines, tasks, instructions, plans, and inside information on how to beat their enemy. The Bible calls this God delivering Israel's enemies into their hands. But sometimes Israel would get a little caught up in the hoopla of everything and turn their back on God. Then they would be defeated, and He would have to come rescue them.

The Israelites possessed something called the ark of the covenant. The ark was a chest that was plated in gold that held the ten commandments within it. More importantly than what was within it was what was on top of it. The top of the ark was called the mercy seat, and it was where the presence of God rested.

One day the Israelites went into a battle with a group called the Philistines. It's important to know that the Philistines weren't some run-of-the-mill little army;

they were powerful and super equipped for battle. They were the first group in Canaan to work with iron, so they had helmets, shields, swords—you get the picture. They weren't an unprepared bunch. Now, I don't know if the Israelites got cocky, if they were outnumbered, if they underestimated their opponent, or if they disobeyed God's instructions, but I do know they lost. And they lost bad.

> And the word of Samuel came to all Israel. Now Israel went out to battle against the Philistines. They encamped at Ebenezer, and the Philistines encamped at Aphek. The Philistines drew up in line against Israel, and when the battle spread, Israel was defeated before the Philistines, who killed about four thousand men on the field of battle.
>
> —1 SAMUEL 4:1–2

Because God had delivered their enemies into their hands so many times, similar to an easy delivery pizza, they couldn't understand why God let them lose this time. So they sent some guys to go pick up the ark of the covenant from a place called Shiloh and bring it back to their camp. They thought the ark would protect them from the Philistines and win the battle for them, because in the past, when the ark was brought into battle, they won.

As you can imagine, when it got there, all of Israel started to cheer and celebrate—they thought they were for sure going to win. They were so loud that the Philistines heard them, and they thought a god had been brought into the camp, meaning either they would die or become slaves.

> The Philistines were afraid, for they said, "A god has come into the camp." And they said, "Woe to us! For nothing like this has happened before. Woe to us! Who can deliver us from the power of these mighty gods? These are the gods who struck the Egyptians with every sort of plague in the wilderness. Take courage, and be men, O Philistines, lest you become slaves to the Hebrews as they have been to you; be men and fight.
> —1 Samuel 4:7–9

... and fight did they ever. The Philistines didn't just fight the Israelites, they slaughtered them, and they took the ark of the covenant with them.

> And did they ever fight! It turned into a rout. They thrashed Israel so mercilessly that the Israelite soldiers ran for their lives, leaving behind an incredible thirty thousand dead. As if that wasn't bad enough, the Chest of God was taken and the two sons of Eli—Hophni and Phinehas—were killed.
> —1 Samuel 4:10–11, The Message

So why did God let them lose? They were His chosen people; they had the ark that carried His presence. Had He abandoned them? No, God didn't abandon them, but He did let them lose. Perhaps the Israelites lost the first small battle because they just didn't prepare well; that can happen in war. When you underestimate the strength of your enemy, you can be defeated. It is just fact.

When they lost the small battle, the Israelites made a vital mistake that cost them the big one: they never asked God for help. They knew they needed His presence to win, but instead of asking God where they went wrong in the initial battle and how they could move forward to receive victory in the retaliation, they just went and got the ark. They relied on what worked previously instead of asking what would work now. What has worked in the past won't always work in the present or future. The ark was powerless without God's presence. A king is not in a position of power because he sits on a throne; a throne is a position of power because it has a king who sits on it. The Israelites stopped focusing on the king and started focusing on the throne, not realizing that a throne is nothing without a king upon it. They might as well have gone and picked up a loaf of bread.

---

**TWEET ABOUT IT!**

God is a God of restoration, so if we must lose, He will always restore what we lost in a greater way when we had it. **#FIERCEHOPE**

---

God still loved them, He had still chosen them, and He still desired their victory. But there are consequences both in life and war when we take our eyes off of God. There is no hope in war if we are not looking to the One who can deliver us through it. It wasn't until later, when the Israelites turned their attention back toward God and cried out to Him to help them, that He delivered them from the Philistines, returned the ark, and restored all that they had lost in the meantime. (See 1 Samuel 7.) God doesn't wish to make us lose and suffer, but He will allow it if it points us back to Him. He is a God of restoration, so if we must lose, He will always restore what we lost in a greater way than when we had it.

## OUR HOPE

The world says that our hope in the midst of war is weapon systems. It says that we should hope in what has worked in the past to work in the future. It tells us that, win or lose, we should stick to our strategies and plans without adjustment. It tells us that our hope should be in leaders who can arm missiles and launch attacks.

Our hope in the midst of war is that God is with us in our victories and in our defeats. He raises up men and women who can defeat armies even if all odds are stacked against them. God gives us plans and blueprints to defeat our enemies. He lines them up to be delivered into our hands. In seasons where we take our eyes off Him and become defeated, He is ready and waiting for us to cry out to Him for help so that He can return victory to us and restore all that we lost. He never leaves us or abandons us.

*Father God, I pray for every person on this planet who is a victim of war right now. I pray that You would protect them, deliver them, heal them.*

*I thank You for the brave men and women who have fought and have given their all, some even their lives, to protect us. Restore to them and their families tenfold what they lost.*

*I rebuke the enemy and his plan to keep servicemen and servicewomen bound by stress and darkness. Send people into their lives to be shoulders and hearts to lean on.*

*Thank You for being with us in victory and defeat. Help us turn our eyes back to You so that we might win every battle and see every victory. I pray that in the moments we see defeat, we would know Your love all the more.*

*In Jesus's name, amen.*

# HOPE IN DEATH

*Because the battle's been fought and the victory won.*
*This fool will not win; his time it will come.*

DEATH IS THE most painful of all eight of the topics covered in this book because all the other seven point to this one. Environmentalism causes death. Natural disasters cause death. Prejudice causes death. Slavery causes death. Genocide causes death. Terrorism causes death. War causes death. Every point in life is summed up in a moment of death.

Physically death is our end. We all have felt the painful effects of death. Whether we have lost a friend, buried a family member, or loved people through unimaginable losses of their own, none of us have been outside the reach of death.

Death is a touchy topic. It is a hard one to cover. I won't be the person who tries to explain the reason you had five miscarriages. I won't be the person who tells you that there was a reason your six-year-old son drowned in a pool he'd swam in nearly every day of his life. I won't be the person who tries to rationalize why you were both in the car, but she died and you didn't. I won't be the one who acts as if your dad dying wasn't the most painful blow of your existence. I just won't. In fact, I can't. Because I don't know. I don't know why those things happened.

## WALKING WITH FRIENDS THROUGH GRIEF

I think that death, especially for a believer, is the greatest test of faith and will to continue. It brings relational tension, financial strain, heartbreak, confusion, doubt, anger, and frustration, and it puts us in a vulnerable state of awareness about the fragility of life. It is important that we work through these ourselves and allow others to work through them as well, so that we can move forward in a healthy way.

I am not now, nor have I ever been, the kind of person or pastor who says, "God has a plan in this," to someone who is confused and grieving. I am not about to tell anyone that God was the reason their kid died. Even if He might have been, I am not about to say it. Nope. I think as believers we need to deal with death realistically and rationally, but we also need to be empathetic and tender.

In the Bible, whenever someone died, oftentimes the family members or friends would cry and mourn; I mean really mourn—rip their shirts off and rub their faces in the dirt and scream mourn. But as soon as they finished, they made sure to secure a burial place and then move forward in a healthy way from there. No one ever made them feel weird about taking time to mourn. We need to make sure that we don't make people feel uncomfortable or as if they are lacking in spiritual understanding or discipline just because they want to take time to mourn.

The Bible says, "Rejoice with those who rejoice, weep with those who weep" (Rom. 12:15). Nothing makes me want to bop a person in the head more than watching a believer try to use the deceased's new home in heaven to rush the mourning process. Yes, Joe is in heaven, but he is also absent from his wife, so slow your roll.

Believer or not, there is a lesson we can learn from this. We need to cry with people. We need to let them mourn.

## THE ENEMY'S ROLE IN DEATH

We don't have to slap a brave face on and act as if death doesn't hurt us. We don't have to act as if we can't be sad because God is sovereign. We can be real and raw when death invades our circumstances. That said, it is important to know that death is more than just circumstance; it's an enemy—our ultimate enemy, to be exact—and it will devour every life that we allow it to. The Bible says that Christ "won't let up until the last enemy is down—and the very last enemy is death!" (1 Cor. 15:26, THE MESSAGE).

---

**TWEET ABOUT IT!**

I will rejoice with those who rejoice, and weep with those who weep. See Romans 12:15. #FIERCEHOPE

---

Now, I don't want you thinking that I am saying that death is like the grim reaper or anything. Death isn't some *Final Destination*-acting, scythe-holding, black-coat-wearing psycho roaming around collecting souls as his day job. It's not that kind of enemy. That kind of depiction of death is a joke, and it plays on the fear and emotions of vulnerable human hearts.

The real enemy called death is much more real and much worse. Because even though death is a continual recurrence in nature, it is not natural for us. Just as He created Adam and Eve in the garden, God created us to be whole and unified, living forever in relationship with Him. Death comes in the way of that by way of sin.

## THE PAYMENT FOR SIN AND DEATH

We talked in the first chapter about how sin separates us from God and why that results in bad things happening in the world; we also talked about how sin must be paid for in order to restore our relationship with God. What we didn't talk about was *how* sin gets paid for.

This book ends right where it begins—at the Fall in the garden. When Adam and Eve fell and sin entered the world, it brought death and separation from God. God lives outside of death, reigning forever in eternity. Just as we talked about in chapter 1, when we remain outside of Him, in spiritual death, we live in a metaphorical cage separating us from Him in life. When we remain outside of Him, in physical death, we will forever be in an eternity of torment separating us from Him in death.

Death must be defeated in life *and* in death in order

for us to regain our perfect union with God. However, that is a battle that we alone are unable to win. Sin and death can only be defeated by death itself—an atoning sacrifice, a pure, unadulterated, spotless gift of life to cover sin. Up until Adam and Eve fell, they ran around as naked as jaybirds. They didn't care. When sin entered the world, they felt shame and hid from God. So God killed an animal and made coverings for Adam and Eve. This is the first example in the Bible of death occurring to cover sin.

In the Old Testament that atoning sacrifice was often made with a lamb or calf. Read about it below:

> Therefore not even the first covenant was inaugurated without blood. For when every commandment of the law had been declared by Moses to all the people, he took the blood of calves and goats, with water and scarlet wool and hyssop, and sprinkled both the book itself and all the people, saying, "This is the blood of the covenant that God commanded for you." And in the same way he sprinkled with the blood both the tent and all the vessels used in worship. Indeed, under the law almost everything is purified with blood, and without the shedding of blood there is no forgiveness of sins.
>
> —HEBREWS 9:18–22

The problem with the animal method, though, was that those sacrifices only covered the sin; they did not remove it. Since man would continue to miss the mark and live sinfully, sacrifices would continue to be needed. This lasted for a long time, and then, fortunately for us,

God sent us a permanent solution. That solution came in the person of Jesus. Not just for me, but also for you and for other every person too.

The Bible says that we have all sinned and fallen short of the standard God set before us (Rom. 3:23). Jesus paid the price for our sin:

> But the fact is, it was our pains he carried—our disfigurements, all the things wrong with us. We thought he brought it on himself, that God was punishing him for his own failures. But it was our sins that did that to him, that ripped and tore and crushed him—our sins! He took the punishment, and that made us whole. Through his bruises we get healed. We're all like sheep who've wandered off and gotten lost. We've all done our own thing, gone our own way. And God has piled all our sins, everything we've done wrong, on him, on him. He was beaten, he was tortured, but he didn't say a word. Like a lamb taken to be slaughtered and like a sheep being sheared, he took it all in silence. Justice miscarried, and he was led off—and did anyone really know what was happening? He died without a thought for his own welfare, beaten bloody for the sins of my people. They buried him with the wicked, threw him in a grave with a rich man, even though he'd never hurt a soul or said one word that wasn't true. Still, it's what God had in mind all along, to crush him with pain. The plan was that he give himself as an offering for sin so that he'd see life come from it—life, life, and more life. And God's plan will deeply prosper through him. Out of that terrible travail of soul, he'll see that it's worth it and be glad he did it. Through

what he experienced, my righteous one, my ser-
vant, will make many "righteous ones," as he himself carries the burden of their sins. Therefore, I'll
reward him extravagantly—the best of everything,
the highest honors—because he looked death in
the face and didn't flinch, because he embraced the
company of the lowest. He took on his own shoulders the sin of the many, he took up the cause of
all the black sheep.
—Isaiah 53:4–12, The Message

God sent His Son to pay for sin and to die so that
we wouldn't have to. He sent an innocent, spotless lamb
to lay His life down, though He had no fault of His
own. He came in the form of a baby and lived a sinless, perfect life. His was the most valuable life to ever
be laid down, so that sin was no longer just covered. It
was completely erased. Here is an explanation of His
sacrifice:

For if the blood of goats and bulls, and the sprin-
kling of defiled persons with the ashes of a heifer,
sanctify for the purification of the flesh, how much
more will the blood of Christ, who through the
eternal Spirit offered himself without blemish to
God, purify our conscience from dead works to
serve the living God. Therefore he is the mediator
of a new covenant, so that those who are called
may receive the promised eternal inheritance, since
a death has occurred that redeems them from the
transgressions committed under the first covenant.
—Hebrews 9:13–15

Jesus took on our sin, and He died the most painful, slow, and degrading death. He was crucified on a cross. At that time death by crucifixion was considered the most embarrassing and shameful death a person could have. It was reserved for the lowest and most disgusting criminals. Here is an explanation of how Jesus gave His life for you and for me:

> Then the soldiers of the governor took Jesus into the governor's headquarters, and they gathered the whole battalion before him. And they stripped him and put a scarlet robe on him, and twisting together a crown of thorns, they put it on his head and put a reed in his right hand. And kneeling before him, they mocked him, saying, "Hail, King of the Jews!" And they spit on him and took the reed and struck him on the head. And when they had mocked him, they stripped him of the robe and put his own clothes on him and led him away to crucify him.... And when they had crucified him, they divided his garments among them by casting lots. Then they sat down and kept watch over him there. And over his head they put the charge against him, which read, "This is Jesus, the King of the Jews." Then two robbers were crucified with him, one on the right and one on the left.
>
> —Matthew 27:27–31, 35–38

I can't even read the story without getting torn up. Insert weeping emojis here, for real. I can picture every moment: when they beat Him, when they smashed the thorns into His head, when they forced Him to carry His cross up the hill, when they drove the nails through His hands and feet, when they pierced His side with a spear. I can imagine it so vividly. Probably because I know I deserve to be there. Every gash, every wound, and every thorn bore my name. Think of every horrible thing in your life. Think of every moment you have missed the mark. Each time you hurt someone or hurt yourself, He wore that hurt on the cross for you.

## CONQUERING DEATH

Really, if Jesus just died for us, this would be a moving story, but it is so much more than that! He didn't just die; He beat death. Our hope is not found in His death but in the fact that He used death to conquer death. He didn't stay dead. He got up!

> When the Sabbath was past, Mary Magdalene, Mary the mother of James, and Salome bought spices, so that they might go and anoint him. And very early on the first day of the week, when the sun had risen, they went to the tomb. And they were saying to one another, "Who will roll away the stone for us from the entrance of the tomb?" And looking up, they saw that the stone had been rolled back— it was very large. And entering the tomb, they saw a young man sitting on the right side, dressed in a white robe, and they were alarmed. And he said to them, "Do not be alarmed. You seek Jesus of Nazareth, who was crucified. *He has risen; he is not here.* See the place where they laid him."
>
> —MARK 16:1–6

That is the hope! In the phrase "He has risen; he is not here" we find the fiercest hope that has ever existed.

When Jesus died on the cross that day, death claimed Him and celebrated for three days. For three days the enemy thought he had won; he thought that we would forever be separated from God by sin and death, but then Christ got up. On the third day Christ kicked in the gates of hell and took back the keys so that death could no longer have us. That is our hope, my friends: in Christ, death can no longer have us. We no longer belong to death but to life. In Christ we no longer owe a debt to death. It has been paid in full, and we have life forever and ever.

> ## TWEET ABOUT IT!
> The phrase "He has risen; he is not here" contains the fiercest hope that exists. #FIERCEHOPE

## TO LIVE IS CHRIST, TO DIE IS GAIN

Australian native Andrew Chan and the eight other members of the Bali Nine drug smuggling gang were arrested in 2005 for trying to smuggle heroin from Australia to Indonesia. In many places smuggling drugs would only get you a hefty prison sentence, but not much else. In Indonesia, however, it is an act punishable by the death penalty. The government estimates that thirty-three people die of drug-related issues each day in Indonesia, so they are fiercely cracking down on it. Chan and the rest of the Bali Nine sat on death row for ten years.[1]

While in prison many of the gang were rehabilitated—Chan more so than anyone. He became a pastor within the prison, working on a certification from Harvest Bible College and leading both an English-language church service and a Bible study while there.[2] He applied for clemency and tried to appeal his conviction, citing his rehabilitation, but even with that and protests from around the world, the Indonesian government did not budge and upheld the execution date.

On April 29, 2015, he and the other men were marched outside and lined up in a single file line. As he was led out to where the execution would take place, Chan could be heard asking God to forgive the men who were going to execute them and praying for Indonesia. When it came time to face the firing squad, he and the other men declined blindfolds and instead courageously faced their executors directly. The men recited the Lord's Prayer, embraced one another, and then, to everyone's surprise, began to sing.[3]

The men made it through the entire first verse of Matt Redman's song "10,000 Reasons (Bless the Lord)," but halfway through the second verse the executioners opened fire and killed them. Andrew Chan praised God up until his last moment, even facing death.[4]

He not only accepted his death but also celebrated that he would be with Christ in heaven soon. When his final appeal to overturn his death penalty was turned down, he said this:

> When I got back to my cell, I said, "God, I asked
> you to set me free, not kill me." God spoke to me
> and said, "Andrew, I have set you free from the
> inside out, I have given you life!" From that moment
> on I haven't stopped worshipping Him.[5]

Chan realized what the apostle Paul also realized when he wrote "To live is Christ, and to die is gain" (Phil. 1:21). They each understood that death in Christ offered them something far greater than life itself. For the unbeliever death is something to fear. For the believer death is not the moment we stop being alive, but it is the moment that we go from being alive to truly living—living the way we were intended to live, in whole, perfect communion with Christ. Because of this, death is no longer something to mourn, but it is something to celebrate because it means we are now with God. We are free from pain, free from suffering, free from loss, and free from sin:

> "O death, where is your victory? O death, where is
> your sting?" The sting of death is sin and the power
> of sin is the law. But thanks be to God, who gives
> us the victory through our Lord Jesus Christ.
> —1 CORINTHIANS 15:55–57

## LIFE THROUGH HIS DEATH

I wrote this spoken word for Easter. I never posted it. I didn't feel peace about it, which was kind of bummer because I worked hard on it and didn't understand why God would have me write something that would stay stored and untouched in my phone. It was while I was

writing this chapter that God spoke to me and told me
to finally use it, and I am so glad He had me wait. His
timing is so perfect.

> With whips and their fists Jesus's body they
>     maimed.
> They stripped Him and beat Him and clothed
>     Him in shame.
> A purple robe on His shoulders, a crown of thorns
>     on His head,
> They didn't care who He was; they wanted Him
>     dead.
> "Hail, King of the Jews!" was what they would
>     shout
> As they sent Him to die and silence their doubt.
> They delivered Him up, like food on a platter.
> They called for His death for His life did not
>     matter.
> If He is the Savior, the King of us all,
> Will God let Him die? Will He let His Son fall?
> They gave Him the chance to prove them all
>     wrong,
> But He didn't budge; He knew all along
> This was His fate, it was part of the plan.
> But as divine as He was, He was also a man.
> So I wonder was He scared or in pain or just mad.
> Was He hurt the God who did this was also His
>     dad?
> If He was He didn't show it, He was solid and
>     quiet.
> He stood and He waited and they started to riot.
> Then they called for the worst—a death so
>     degrading

It was reserved for murderers and those long past
  saving.
This wasn't fair; in fact, it's unjustified
That an innocent man would be crucified.
To a place called Golgotha, He carried His cross.
Crowds followed behind Him, mourning their loss.
For they knew who He was, the one true Messiah.
He wasn't a faker and He wasn't a liar.
With one nail in His feet and two in His hands
He shouted, "Father, forgive them; they don't
  understand."
There on skull hill He hung arms open wide,
Then a guard took a spear, and he pierced His side.
Onlookers watched and religious men scoffed,
"If You are God's son, come down from that cross!"
But Jesus hung still; on that tree He would stay.
Death was already coming, He would not turn it
  away.
A sign over His head read "King of the Jews."
It was made as a joke; if only they knew
That it wasn't a joke and it wasn't a game.
He was that man, He did bear that name.
Though it was noon, the whole world grew dark.
Then Jesus stirred on the cross and made a remark:
"God, why have You left Me, where have You
  gone?"
And He breathed His last as the people looked on.
They mocked and they spat and they left Him for
  dead.
They thought it was finished when low hung His
  head.
So down came His body, and they wrapped it in
  linen

To conceal and to cover all the wounds He'd been
    given.
He was sealed in a tomb by a door made of stone,
Laid flat on a rock with no crown or a throne.
Satan was pleased; he thought he was winning.
But this isn't the end, it's just the beginning.
For three days darkness won and death celebrated.
But on the third day it all culminated
With this, the moment, the point of the story.
It wasn't His death that brings God the glory.
On Sunday they saw the stone rolled away
Revealing the tomb was empty that day.
Christ was not there; He rose from that grave.
His death wasn't for nothing; our souls it did save.
He'd conquered hell, He now had the keys.
Death was defeated—taken out at the knees.
Christ dead and lifeless as He hung on the cross,
Crushed, broken, and beaten. He did this for us.
Every gash, every cut, it was me on His mind.
He bore the sin on His shoulders for all of
    mankind.
While we were still filthy, He hung on a tree.
He bled and He died for you and for me.
Because sin demands payment, it comes with a
    cost.
We owed a debt, our freedom He bought.
His body the payment, His blood paid the price,
Given wholly and freely, a pure sacrifice.
He took my guilt, my sin, and my shame.
Because of His love I'm no longer the same.
Every hurt, every heartbreak, ever tear that I've
    cried,
Every dark dirty secret that I keep deep inside,

He saw and He knew and still thought me worthy.
He doesn't think that I'm gross, He doesn't think I
    am dirty.
When Christ hung on the cross, He did more than
    just die.
With that act of love He disproved a lie
That death is the end, that darkness will reign
That regardless of trying, we'll end up in pain.
There is more to this life than just growing old.
Don't settle for small, like you've always been told.
I know it gets hard, but those voices must hush.
We were worth more; life was given for us.
Don't live in frustration and bound up in strife.
The Son of a King thought us worthy of life.
The road between us and life He did mend,
And seeing us now…He'd do it again.

---

### TWEET ABOUT IT

The day death died, fierce hope was born.
**#FIERCEHOPE**

---

## OUR HOPE

The world says that there is no hope in death. It says that death is the end. The world says that once your time card is stamped and you are on the way out, there is nothing more for you. The world gives us no hope for more, no option for eternity, no direction for life. It says that an expensive funeral and a nice headstone are the only treasures you can look forward to. Man, the world is so wrong.

Our hope in the midst of death is that death has been defeated and is no longer the period at the end of the sentence, separating us from God! God loves us so much that He sent His only Son to give His life and pay for our sins so that we wouldn't have to. When Christ hung on the cross, He defeated death, hell, and the grave. All we have to do is accept Him, and then we are no longer bound by sin and death! The day death died, fierce hope was born.

*Father God, I am hurting because of death. Heal the wounds and scars that death has left on my heart.*

*I ask that You would comfort everyone else who is dealing with pain from death. God, I thank You for sending Your Son, Jesus, to the cross in my place. I owed a debt that I could not pay, and He paid a debt that He did not owe. Thank You for that.*

*I ask that You remove fear of death in my life. I am not afraid of death anymore, and I rebuke the enemy's plan to keep me in fear. I thank You that Christ didn't just die, but that He got up.*

*In Jesus's name, amen.*

# 10

# THE HOPE OF THE WORLD

*But hear what I say—there is peace in the end.*
*It's coming so quickly, it's right 'round the bend.*

I WANT TO SHARE my heart with you for a minute before we wrap up this journey of finding hope together. Here is a secret for you: I wanted to quit writing this book. More than once, actually. I cried and yelled and fought my husband when he encouraged me not to quit. By the time I got to this chapter, I was so empty and drained that I wanted to just send it in blank.

The truth is I have never done anything more difficult than write this book, and I have given birth to two children without pain medication. God orchestrated it in such a way that what normally takes more than a year took barely more than a few weeks—a few really hard weeks. I didn't spend time with many people, and if I was spending time with them, it was obvious my thoughts were somewhere else. My sleep was short and sporadic. My husband and kids would go to bed, and I would stay up for hours and hours and write while my half of the world was asleep. Without my husband to watch our boys day in and day out to free me up to do this, it would never have been done. I thought of reasons, valid reasons, to stop on more than one occasion. In writing this book, I learned to survive each day on one Lean Cuisine meal, two-hour bursts of sleep, and three cups of coffee.

I have fought the enemy tooth and nail every step of the way. I fought sickness when I hadn't been sick for months, pain when I had no reason to feel pain, financial struggles that had never been an issue before, stress in relationships that had been dealt with and over long before this book began, and distraction after distraction that would cause even the most well-rested, calm, focused person to lose his mind. The enemy pulled out every stop, and sometimes he nearly got me. I dealt with issues in my heart that I thought hadn't been issues in years. I had every feeling of inadequacy and insecurity known to man. I constantly fought the thoughts that said I wasn't good enough, educated enough, or soft enough. I felt, again and again, that I wouldn't have enough to say to fill these pages. I was continually faced with the enemy rubbing my insecurities in my face as if they were some kind of disqualifier.

I have wanted to be a writer since I was five or six years old—literally as long as I can remember. My entire life I dreamed that I would get to see the call of God, the desire of my heart, and the hope of my life become a reality—that I would become an author. But I had no idea that it would be like this. I imagined the scenario a million times, and it never looked like the one that played out.

Of every idea I've ever had and for every book I could have written, I will never understand why it had to be this one. I could have written a hilarious satire about the woes of motherhood. I could have written a challenging call to action for wives and their husbands. I could have written a moving story about God making your dreams come true when you least expect it, but instead I wrote this: a painful, controversial, heartbreaking, hard book. I wrote a book about hope but containing topics that are each hard and confusing enough to write an entire book about each of them as individuals. It has been an exhilarating, emotional, lightning bolt of an experience. And knowing what I know now—having experienced the journey, having walked the road that nearly killed me—if I could go back and undo the steps that led me here, I wouldn't.

I wouldn't change it for a million book deals. Not for a moment.

There has never been a thing in my life that I have done or that I believe in more than this book. I have never filled the pages of anything with as many tears and prayers as I did this book. I have never leaned on God more than I did while writing this book. I have never poured out my heart more than I did in these pages. And that is because there is not a thing on this earth that I believe in more than the hope that is in this book.

## HOPE IS REAL

I will never understand why I am sitting alone at my table, safe in my South Florida apartment, thanking

God for all the blessings my family and I have while my children and husband sleep soundly in their beds, and across the world there is a mother just like me sitting at her table in Syria, begging God to spare her life and the lives of her husband and children. I will never understand why, during the weeks I was writing this book, there were more than forty thousand people in Louisiana who lost everything they owned in floods that happened in areas that weren't even flood zones. Many families lost not only their homes but also every picture, every memory, and every prize when floodwaters rose inch by inch, enveloping every precious memory that they hold dear. I will never understand or be able to comprehend the hearts of men and women behind acts of violence so despicable that my stomach churns just reading about them. I will never understand why I was born a free woman in the twentieth century and not a slave woman in the nineteenth century. I can't explain why tornados land where they land or why murderers kill whom they kill.

I can't answer any of those questions, and frankly this book wasn't meant to do that. It was simply meant to point people toward hope when hope seems pointless.

The world can be a dark, scary place, and it needs hope now more than ever. There is not a day that goes by that I don't turn on the news or look at my phone to see heartbreak and devastation wrecking the world.

The enemy is working overtime to keep us separated from God and bound by death. But I believe this book points us to the tools and perspective to keep hope out in front of us. We can live our lives carrying hope every day instead of being tossed back and forth by the circumstances around us.

> ## TWEET ABOUT IT
> Hope is a person, and His name is Jesus.
> **#FIERCEHOPE**

God tells us in His Word that where sin grows greatly, grace grows even greater (Rom. 5:20). I believe that the same can be said about the hope we find in Christ as well. Wherever you find tragedy and loss and pain beyond compare, you will also find the hope of God flooding in changing lives and healing hearts. That may look like relief workers from many different nations and organizations bringing supplies and food to disaster zones, such as when Haiti was devastated by an earthquake. Or it may look like a boot kicking in a door to arrest human traffickers and rescue those who would have no hope, such as the movement that began when a small Greek woman from Australia was moved with hurt and urgency over the slavery crisis in our world.

Hope comes in many different forms, but the reality is that when all hope seems lost and circumstances are beyond logical solutions, a hope that is more than a feeling and more than a momentary mood change walks in and changes everything. That hope is a person, and His name is Jesus. This may seem like a cheesy, Christian oversimplification of things; however, it is powerfully, awesomely true! When you have experienced such hope, you understand it. There is nothing like watching Jesus walk in and bring hope into your life, a hope so fierce that it overcomes any situation and hurt.

## HOPE IN DIFFICULT CIRCUMSTANCES

If environmentalism is a passion in your life or a fear in your life causing you to live every day stressed out about limited resources and worry that the world cannot sustain us forever, I want you to know that there is hope. It is my prayer for you that you would find hope in the supernatural provision of God who creates, sustains, and supplies everything in existence.

If you have experienced the devastation of a natural disaster or if you live in constant concern that the next storm could rob you of your life or all of your belongings, I want you to know that there is hope. It is my prayer for you that you find hope in the sovereignty of God and peace in the knowledge that He can stop the storm at any time, and if He doesn't, He is still in the storm with you.

If you are enraged by prejudice and feel as if you are powerless to make real changes even though you have done everything you can to be a social-justice warrior and civil-rights activist, I want you to know there is hope. It is my prayer for you that you find hope in a God who bought all bloods with His blood and sees no color. I pray that you are encouraged that Christ cared about tearing down barriers long before you did.

If slavery breaks your heart and you feel the burden of every life in chains and are desperate to see the enslaved set free, I want you to know that there is hope. It is my prayer that you would find hope in the fact that Jesus paid the highest price for the freedom of every person on this planet, and He desires just as much as you do to see them saved and set free.

If genocide makes you sick to your stomach and you are so upset by it that you cannot figure out how to put humanity back in focus for both the victim and abuser, I want you to know there is hope. It is my prayer for you that you find hope in the God who freely gave forgiveness to us and empowers us to forgive others too. Remember that no one is so broken that He cannot fix them.

If you find yourself frightened to travel and live your life because of the threat of terrorism, or if you are living bound with the pain from a terrorist attack that affected you directly, I want you to know that there is hope. It is my prayer that you find hope in God's ability to wreck religion, seek relationship, and change every heart, no matter how hardened it is. He can bring healing to any wound, no matter how old.

If you feel the hardship of war, directly or indirectly, and are still struggling with adjusting in the life you live now, I want you to know that there is hope. It is my prayer that you find hope in a God who is with us in both victory and defeat. Hold tight to a God who can deliver our enemy right into our hands.

If you live bound by the fear of death because of the loss of a loved one or because you are simply afraid to die, I want you to know there is hope. It is my prayer that you find hope in the God who defeated death, hell, and the grave and gave us the keys to reign freely with Him forever.

## FIERCE HOPE

The hope that is found in these topics is real, true hope, but they are also smaller portions of hope that comes from a much larger source. Fierce hope comes from the God who fills these pages—a sovereign, loving, merciful, just, kind, compassionate, sacrificial Father who loves us so much that He gave us a way out of every scenario in this book and a million others that we cannot even fathom. And He gives so much more than just hope. He gives provision that makes no sense to the logical mind. He gives love that bridges every divide. He gives peace that passes all understanding. He gives wisdom that transcends every thought. He gives healing that fixes every wound. He is all things to all men. Not because He has to be, but because He wants to be.

Remember in the beginning of the book when I said that I didn't want you to feel pressured to make a decision right away? I said to wait it out if you wanted, hear all the facts, and decide at the end. Well, this is that moment. I don't want you to think that this decision is a quick fix for an easy life, because it's not. I can't promise you that your life won't be hard still. In fact, I can pretty much guarantee that it will be even harder at times. As you move forward, you are going to deal with either environmentalism, natural disasters, slavery, prejudice, genocide, terrorism, war, or death. Some might deal with a few, and even more heartbreaking, a few of you will experience them all.

But if you make a decision to follow Jesus, you will experience these things with a hope so great and peace so strong that you will feel as if you have more to live for in having experienced them than not experiencing them at all. See, His hope cannot be stopped, and it cannot be outdone. This hope brings a confidence and foundation in these times of pain or hurt. Jesus will never leave you hanging, and He will never walk out when things get hard, and because of that you never have to live hopeless again.

Many times in my life I have gone through painful or difficult things, and I had hope in those situations. The problem was that hope began to fade as things played out. All my hope was wrapped up in my own solutions or ways that I could fix things myself. I don't know about you, but I hate when I am not in control or when my own ideas don't change my situation. It is a very helpless, frustrating feeling. Many times I have found myself in a situation that I could not plan, work, or talk myself out of. Have you ever had a moment in your life like that, where the pain and problems are real, but no matter how hard you try, you literally can do nothing about it? I have too.

It is in these difficult moments that the fierce hope I have been talking about makes its entrance. God and the fierce hope found in Him is so much better than any hope that I have had in my own abilities or solutions. He is more trustworthy than any government or activist, and He will outlast all disasters or radical religious groups. He is not intimidated by the present circumstances of our world, and He has already seen what our futures hold. He is the only hope that you will have that will not run out or fade. He is the only hope that will not sour or prove itself disloyal. And the craziest part is that He doesn't want to be in your life only when there is tragedy or pain, but He wants to be there every day. He wants to fill your life with joy and purpose so great that it blows your mind. He is fierce hope, and so much more.

### TWEET ABOUT IT!

God is our **#FIERCEHOPE**.

If you want that hope for yourself, that protection and love, that belonging and covering, this is your chance. Wherever you are in life, no matter how far gone you are, He loves you and He wants to give you all of these things. If you are at home reading quietly in your bed, at work reading at your desk, in your car on your lunch break, or flying across the country sandwiched in between two strangers, all you have to do is read and mean the prayer below. It is my favorite prayer I have written in the whole book. You can do it boldly and loudly or quiet and strong. It is up to you. Just do whatever the gentle tugging in your heart says to do.

*Father God, I need You.*
    *I realize that I am a sinner in need of a Savior.*
*I believe that You died and rose for me.*

*I turn away from the person I used to be. For-
give me for everything I have ever done before
now.*

*I want You to come into my heart and change
my life. From the bottom to the top, take out
every bad thing and fill it with You.*

*I need You. I believe in You. I trust You.*

*In Jesus's name, amen.*

That's literally it. It is all you have to do, and then
He is there. I always feel so silly when I do this part
because it is so simple. There is no special trick or ritual.

He wants to be with you, He wants to be close to you,
He wants to make every desire of your heart and hope
for your life come true, and He made it as simple as
inviting Him to come do it. When you say that prayer,
the old version of you is dead and gone, and you have
found new life in Christ. It doesn't matter who you
were five minutes ago or five years ago. In that moment
you become a new creation.

If you found new life today, I want to challenge you
do to three things: Shout it. Solidify it. Share it. These
three things will help position you in the best place
possible to get the most of your new life and decision.

Shout it is my favorite of the three things I want you
to do, because this one involves me. One of my favorite
things to do is dance and celebrate the moment of life
change that you experienced when you said this prayer.
Send me a shout out on Twitter, Facebook, or Instagram
that says this: "Hey, Savanna Hartman, celebrate with
me. I just found #FierceHope!"

This way I can easily find you and celebrate with you. I want you to know that wherever I am, in public or private, I will celebrate right there the moment I read it.

The second thing I want you to do is find a church and get involved somewhere. Fierce hope is strengthened—supercharged if you will—by being in community with other believers. Don't feel like you have to get yourself perfect before you are accepted at church. If the church you visit or attend makes you feel as if you aren't good enough, find a new church.

Be bold and step out. I know it's hard, but the reward is great. Remember, the enemy wants to keep you separated and isolated. Many people go to a church and then leave because they feel that no one pays them any attention. Don't do that. If you don't feel seen, introduce yourself to someone and make sure they see you. Get plugged into a connect group, small group, men or women's ministry, or some other area you can grow in accountability, friendship, strength, and celebration. Life is better in circles. Don't do life alone.

The third thing I want you to do is to share it. One of the most important things, if not the most important thing, that we need to do when we accept Christ is share it. Share it with anyone who will listen. Think about it: if you just received the most incredible gift, you would tell everyone and show it off as much as you can! Think of this the same way.

Something really awesome happens when we profess (which is just a fancy word for talk about) accepting the fierce hope of Christ into our lives. We begin to root our decision into our heart, and it begins to shape our identity. Your identity is shaped by what you talk about, so talk about this! Carry the hope you have received into the world around you. Give someone a copy of this book. Invite them to church. Pray for that stranger in the supermarket. Share it. It really will change your life. Plus, and trust me on this, it gets really fun. One of my favorite things to do in life is carry this hope and place it in the hands of hurting people.

If this isn't you, if you read the whole book and you're still not sure, that is OK. I still love you, and I am thankful that you read it all and allowed the seed to be planted in your heart. But I want to leave you with this, the last line of the spoken word that this entire book is framed around:

> You might think I'm crazy and that this isn't true,
> But with the way the world is, what have you to
> lose?

# NOTES

### CHAPTER 1—THE HURT OF THE WORLD

1. "Suicide Facts," Suicide Awareness Voices of Education, accessed August 29, 2016, http://www.save.org/index.cfm?fuseaction=home.viewPage&page_id=705D5DF4-055B-F1EC-3F66462866FCB4E6.

### CHAPTER 2—HOPE IN ENVIRONMENTALISM

1. "About John," Planet Walk, accessed August 29, 2016, http://planetwalk.org/about-john/; John Francis, "Walk the Earth...My 17-Year Vow of Silence," transcript, Ted Talks, November 2008, accessed August 24, 2016, https://www.ted.com/talks/john_francis_walks_the_earth/transcript?language=en.

2. Edward Humes, *Garbology: Our Dirty Love Affair With Trash* (New York: Penguin Group, 2012).

3. "Recycling Facts," The University of Utah: College of Architecture and Planning, accessed August 29, 2016, http://students.arch.utah.edu/courses/Arch4011/Recycling%20Facts1.pdf.

4. "The World's Worst Pollution Problems: The Top Ten of the Toxic Twenty," Green Cross, Blacksmith Institute, 2008, accessed August 29, 2016, http://www.greencross.ch/uploads/media/pollution_report_2008_top_ten_wwpp.pdf.

5. "Deforestation Facts," Conserve Energy Future, accessed August 29, 2016, http://www.conserve-energy-future.com/various-deforestation-facts.php.

6. "Hazardous Waste Statistics," The World Counts, accessed August 29, 2016, http://www.theworldcounts.com/counters/waste_pollution_facts/hazardous_waste_statistics#more-facts.

7. The Ocean Cleanup, accessed August 29, 2016, www.theoceancleanup.com; Boyan Slat, accessed August 24, 2016, www.boyanslat.com.

### CHAPTER 3—HOPE IN NATURAL DISASTER

1. "Hurricane Katrina: A Climatological Perspective," National Oceanic and Atmospheric Administration's National Climatic Data Center, October 2005, updated August 2006, accessed August 29, 2016, http://www.ncdc .noaa.gov/oa/reports/tech-report-200501z.pdf.

2. Ibid.

3. "Natural Disasters Since 1900—Over 8 Million Deaths and 7 Trillion US Dollars Damage," April 18, 2016, accessed August 29, 2016, http://m.phys.org/news/2016-04-natural -disasters-1900over-million-deaths.html.

4. Rick Warren, "God Is an Expert at Bringing Good Out of Bad," Pastor Rick's Daily Hope, May 21, 2014, accessed August 29, 2016, http://pastorrick.com/devotional/english /god-is-an-expert-at-bringing-good-out-of-bad.

### CHAPTER 4—HOPE IN PREJUDICE

1. This interview can be viewed online. Rodney Dunigan, "Tampa Pastor's Emotional Reaction to Alton Sterling Shooting Go Viral," *ABC Action News*, July 7, 2016, accessed September 1, 2016, http://www.abcactionnews .com/news/local-news/tampa-pastors-emotional-reaction -to-alton-sterling-shooting-go-viral.

2. "King, Martin Luther (Michael), Sr. (1897–1984)," Martin Luther King Jr. and the Global Freedom Struggle, Stanford.edu, accessed September 1, 2016, http://king encyclopedia.stanford.edu/encyclopedia/encyclopedia enc_king_martin_luther_michael_sr_1897_1984/; "Martin Luther King Jr.—Biography," Nobel Prize, accessed September 1, 2016, http://www.nobelprize.org/nobel_prizes /peace/laureates/1964/king-bio.html.

3. Martin Luther King Jr., "'Loving Your Enemies,' Sermon Delivered at Dexter Avenue Baptist Church," November 17, 1957, found in Clayborne Carson, ed., *The Papers of Martin Luther King, Jr.: Symbol of the Movement*, volume IV (Los Angeles: University of California Press, 2000), 321–322.

## Chapter 5—Hope in Slavery

1. "Natalia's Story," A21, accessed August 30, 2016, http://www.a21.org/content/natalias-story/gjdpkt?permcode=gjdpkt.

2. Kate Hodal and Chris Kelly, "Trafficked Into Slavery on Thai Trawlers to Catch Food for Prawns," *The Guardian*, June 10, 2014, accessed August 30, 2016, https://www.theguardian.com/global-development/2014/jun/10/-sp-migrant-workers-new-life-enslaved-thai-fishing.

3. Jim Kavanagh, "Human Trafficking: 'Everyone Can Do Something,'" CNN Freedom Project, June 16, 2011, accessed August 30, 2016, http://thecnnfreedomproject.blogs.cnn.com/2011/06/16/abolishing-sex-slavery-by-helping-one-girl-at-a-time/.

4. Brian O'Keefe, "Inside Big Chocolate's Child Labor Problem," *Fortune*, March 1, 2016, accessed August 30, 2016, http://fortune.com/big-chocolate-child-labor/.

5. David Blair, "The World Has Over 45 Million Slaves—Including 1.2 Million in Europe—Finds New Study," *The Telegraph*, May 31, 2016, accessed August 30, 2016, http://www.telegraph.co.uk/news/2016/05/31/the-world-has-over-45-million-slaves---including-12-million-in-e/; Max Fisher, "This Map Shows Where the World's 30 Million Slaves Live. There Are 60,000 in the U.S.," *Washington Post*, October 17, 2013, accessed August 30, 2016, https://www.washingtonpost.com/news/worldviews/wp/2013/10/17/this-map-shows-where-the-worlds-30-million-slaves-live-there-are-60000-in-the-u-s/.

6. "Human Trafficking," A21, accessed August 26, 2016, http://www.a21.org/content/human-trafficking/gl0ryw?permcode=gl0ryw.

7. "A Profitable Enterprise," CNN Freedom Project, July 29, 2011, accessed August 30, 2016, http://thecnnfreedomproject.blogs.cnn.com/2011/07/29/a-profitable-enterprise/; Tony Maddox, "Modern-Day Slavery: A Problem that Can't Be Ignored," CNN Freedom Project, March 4, 2011, accessed August 30, 2016, http://thecnnfreedomproject.blogs.cnn.com/2011/03/04/modern-day-slavery-a-problem-that-cant-be-ignored/.

8. "ILO 2012 Global Estimate of Forced Labour: Executive Summary, International Labour Organization," 2012, accessed August 30, 2016, http://www.ilo.org/wcmsp5 /groups/public/@ed_norm/@declaration/documents /publication/wcms_181953.pdf.

9. Heather Clawson, Nicole Dutch, Amy Solomon, and Lisa Goldblatt Grace, "Human Trafficking Into and Within the United States: A Review of the Literature," Office of the Assistant Secretary for Planning and Evaluation, August 30, 2009, accessed August 30, 2016, https://aspe.hhs.gov /basic-report/human-trafficking-and-within-united-states -review-literature.

10. Ibid.

11. Ibid.

12. Jim Kavanagh, "Abolishing Sex Slavery by Helping One Girl at a Time," CNN, June 16, 2011, accessed August 30, 2016, http://thecnnfreedomproject.blogs.cnn.com/2011 /06/16/abolishing-sex-slavery-by-helping-one-girl-at -a-time/.

13. Ibid.

### CHAPTER 6—HOPE IN GENOCIDE

1. "Hitler Fails Art Exam," The History Place, accessed August 30, 2016, http://www.historyplace.com/worldwar2 /riseofhitler/art.htm.

2. "Hitler Sketches That Failed to Secure His Place at Art Academy to Be Auctioned," *The Telegraph*, March 24, 2010, accessed August 30, 2016, http://www.telegraph.co.uk /culture/art/art-news/7511134/Hitler-sketches-that-failed -to-secure-his-place-at-art-academy-to-be-auctioned.html.

3. "The Rwandan Genocide," History, accessed August 30, 2016, http://www.history.com/topics/rwandan-genocide.

4. Ibid.

5. Ibid.

6. Immaculee Ilibagiza, *Left to Tell: Discovering God Amidst the Rwandan Holocaust* (New York: Hay House, 2006).

7. Ibid.

8. Joe Shute, "Why I Forgave the Nazis Who Murdered My Family," *The Telegraph*, January 20, 2016, accessed August

30, 2016, http://www.telegraph.co.uk/history/world-war
-two/12111155/Why-I-forgive-the-Nazis-who-murdered
-my-family.html; "'It's For You to Know That You Forgive,'
Says Holocaust Survivor," NPR, May 24, 2015, accessed
August 30, 2016, http://www.npr.org/2015/05/24
/409286734/its-for-you-to-know-that-you-forgive-says
-holocaust-survivor.

9. Shute, "Why I Forgave the Nazis Who Murdered My Family."

10. Ibid.

11. "'It's For You to Know That You Forgive,' Says Holocaust Survivor."

### CHAPTER 7—HOPE IN TERRORISM

1. "Nice Attack: At Least 84 Killed by Lorry at Bastille Day Celebrations," BBC News, July 15, 2016, accessed August 30, 2016, http://www.bbc.com/news/world-europe -36800730; Camila Domonoske, "'Sheer Terror' as Attack Along French Riviera Kills at Least 84," NPR, July 15, 2016, accessed August 30, 2016, http://www.npr.org /sections/thetwo-way/2016/07/15/486132294/bastille-day -truck-attack-in-nice-france-what-we-know.

2. Steve Visser, "Death Toll Rises to 85 in Bastille Day Attack in Nice," CNN, August 5, 2016, accessed August 30, 2016, http://www.cnn.com/2016/08/05/europe/nice -france-attack-victim/.

3. Ralph Ellis, Ashley Fantz, Faith Karimi, and Elliot McLaughlin, "Orlando Shooting: 49 Killed, Shooter Pledged ISIS Allegiance," CNN, June 13, 2016, accessed August 30, 2016, http://www.cnn.com/2016/06/12/us /orlando-nightclub-shooting/; James Rothwell, Harriet Alexander, Ruth Sherlock, Raziye Akkoc, and Chris Graham, "Details Emerge About Orlando Gunman Omar Mateen," *The Telegraph*, June 13, 2016, accessed August 30, 2016, http://www.telegraph.co.uk/news/2016/06/14/details -emerge-about-orlando-gunman-omar-mateen/.

4. Oren Dorell, "2016 Already Marred by Nearly Daily Terror Attacks," *USA Today*, July 15, 2016, accessed

August 30, 2016, http://www.usatoday.com/story/news /world/2016/06/29/major-terrorist-attacks-year/86492692/.

## CHAPTER 8—HOPE IN WAR

1. In discussion with author, August 19, 2016.

## CHAPTER 9—HOPE IN DEATH

1. "Bali Nine Ringleaders Andrew Chan and Myuran Suku- maran," BBC, April 29, 2015, accessed August 31, 2016, http://www.bbc.com/news/world-asia-30997099.

2. Ibid.; Jewel Topsfield, "Bali Nine Andrew Chan Com- forted Inmate After He Lost Mercy Plea," *Sydney Morning Herald*, January 23, 2015, accessed August 31, 2016, http:// www.smh.com.au/world/bali-nine-andrew-chan-comforted -inmate-after-he-lost-mercy-plea-20150123-12wxfe.html; Tom Allard, "Faith Sustains Condemned Man Andrew Chan," *Sydney Morning Herald*, June 21, 2011, accessed August 31, 2016, http://www.smh.com.au/national/faith -sustains-condemned-man-andrew-chan-20110620-1gbxk .html#ixzz1RyaPcsxR.

3. Mark Woods, "Andrew Chan Was Executed Singing 10,000 Reasons, Widow Tells Funeral Congregation," *Christianity Today*, May 8, 2015, accessed August 31, 2016, http://www.christiantoday.com/article/andrew.chan.was .executed.singing.10000.reasons.widow.tells.funeral .congregation/53536.htm; Joy Tibbs, "Matt Redman on How Executed Prisoners Sang 10,000 Reasons," June 11, 2015, accessed August 31, 2016, https://www.premier christianity.com/Blog/Matt-Redman-on-how-executed -prisoners-sang-10-000-Reasons.

4. Ibid.

5. Chris Makin, "Following Jesus on Death Row," Eternity News.com, August 2, 2013, accessed August 31, 2016, https://www.eternitynews.com.au/good-news/following -jesus-on-death-row/.

# ABOUT THE AUTHOR

Savanna and her husband, Matt, live in Tampa, FL, with their two sons, August and Atlas. Matt and Savanna moved to Tampa from their hometown in North Florida in spring of 2015 to plant a new church, Banner Church. Together, she and Matt serve as the senior pastors in a rapidly growing ministry that focuses on loving God with their whole heart and loving people with their whole lives. They are passionate about seeing people from every walk of life find hope and belonging, especially those who don't fit the traditional church mold.

Savanna has a heart for social justice and civil rights and has gained international attention for using the art of spoken word poetry to address tough topics ranging from slavery to race relations. She is passionate about seeing all men and women, regardless of their color or creed, live in the freedom that new life in Christ brings. She seeks to live a life that tears down racial, social, economic, and financial barriers that keep people marginalized and stereotyped and prevent them from living feeling loved and respected.

She has been featured all over the nation on both news and radio and has enjoyed watching her platform grow, giving her opportunities to speak at churches and conferences all over the United States.

To give to their ministry, get involved, or find out more information about **Banner Church** please visit: www.banner.church or email: info@banner.church

To have Savanna come speak at your church or event, email **booking@savannahartman.com** You can connect with her here! Instagram: @savannamhartman Facebook: /savannamhartman Twitter: @savannahartman Website: www.savannahartman.com

# CONNECT WITH US!

**CHARISMA HOUSE**

( Spiritual Growth )

f Facebook.com/CharismaHouse

🐦 @CharismaHouse

📷 Instagram.com/CharismaHouseBooks

( Health )

📌 Pinterest.com/CharismaHouse

REALMS
( Fiction )

f Facebook.com/RealmsFiction